＊＊＊

Borderman

＊＊＊

BORDERMAN

Memoirs of
Federico José María Ronstadt

Edited by Edward F. Ronstadt
Foreword by Bernard L. Fontana

A University of Arizona
Southwest Center Book

University of New Mexico Press
Albuquerque

Library of Congress Cataloging in Publication Data

Ronstadt, Federico José María.
Borderman: memoirs of Federico Josâ María Ronstadt/ edited by
Edward F. Ronstadt; foreword by Bernard L. Fontana.—1st ed.
p.   c.m.
"A University of Arizona Southwest Center Book."
Includes bibliographical references and index.
ISBN 0–8263–1462–7
1. Ronstadt, Federico Josâ María,
2. Mexican Americans—Arizona—Tucson—Biography.
3. Tucson (Ariz.)—Biography.
4. Sonora (Mexico: State)—Biography.
I. Ronstadt, Edward F., 1916–
II. Title.
F819.T99M56 1993
979.1'776046872—dc20
93–3853

All photographic illustrations in this volume are deposited in the
Edward F. Ronstadt Collection, which will soon be deposited in the
University of Arizona Special Collections. Several photographs
reproduced here were donated to the Edward F. Ronstadt Collection by
specific individuals and institutions credited in the caption.

To Mary Catherine

Contents

Foreword

Bernard L. Fontana

Federico José María Ronstadt, known throughout most of his life to his legion of Tucson friends simply as Fred Ronstadt, was the exemplar of a borderlands person. In this instance, the border is a line that, since 1854, has separated Sonora from Arizona and thus Mexico from the United States. But as in border regions throughout the world, the men, women, and children who grow up in them and live there manage to devise their own social, cultural, economic, and even political accommodations to match the realities of their daily lives. They are often less constrained by broader regional and national considerations than are their countrymen farther away from either side of the line. Given enough time, border populations evolve a peculiar subculture, frequently with its own language, music, mores, expectations, and world view. Such border subcultures are also partly the result of familial relationships that ignore international boundaries. Kinship bonds, especially among kinsmen in close geographical proximity, remain as strong as those of nationality.

Federico Ronstadt was born in 1868 in the state of Sonora, Mexico. His mother was a Mexican and his father a German who had become a naturalized Mexican citizen. Fred spent his childhood and early adolescence living in Sonora and Baja California. He came to the United States and Arizona Territory as a young man to learn a trade, eventually becoming an American citizen. Fluent in Spanish and English, he was bicultural in outlook. Proud to be an American, he was unashamed of his Mexican heritage. With many relatives, or *parientes,* on both sides of the international boundary, he was at home equally in Mexico and in his adopted country.

There is a flavor of Horatio Alger in the Fred Ronstadt story, but it would be an exaggeration to imply his tale is altogether one of rags to riches. His father was a highly educated man who for much of his life enjoyed considerable political influence and social prestige. His mother, Margarita Redondo, was a member of an extended family whose forebears had arrived in Sonora in the first half of the eighteenth century and who had acquired land and attendant wealth. That such a life—even for nineteenth-century Sonorans of high social status and property—could be harsh and demanding, with death and deprivation commonplace, is one of the images to emerge from the Ronstadt memoirs. Difficulties of existence notwithstanding, Federico Ronstadt's parents respected and fostered literacy and education among their children, and they did their best to provide them with the skills and intellectual tools needed to succeed in their chosen endeavors.

Federico Ronstadt's memoirs largely concern the first forty years of his life. They include the last three decades of the nineteenth century in northwestern Mexico and in southern Arizona. Later portions of his memoirs, including passages that provide details of his Tucson and El Paso business ventures and that describe later visits to San Francisco and Los Angeles, have been omitted here. The information has already appeared in print, or those sections are less cohesive and lack a sense of immediacy that characterizes the major section published in this volume.

These memoirs offer their reader an extraordinary portrait of the culture of northern Sonora and Baja California during the late nineteenth century. No amount of reading in official documents or standard histories can provide this richness of detail and insight. The hardships of mining in Baja California, for example, with Yaqui Indian laborers and primitive means of extracting and hauling ore come to life through Federico's pencilled words. He also brings to life the travails of pearl divers in the Gulf of California and of a black family mining salt in the blinding glare of Isla Carmen.

Turbulence was a hallmark of Sonora in the decades of the 1860s and 1870s. In 1871 Mexico celebrated its first half-century as an independent nation, and during those fifty years political unrest and instability were constant on the far northwestern frontier where various personalities, principally Governor Ignacio Pesqueira and Governor and General Manuel Gándara, competed for political and military control of Sonora.[1] Moreover, Sonora remained a frontier at war with

Apache Indians, at least until the defeat of Geronimo in 1886. Cattlemen, small farmers, prospectors, and miners had to contend with the threat of Indian attack as well as placate opposing Mexican military factions.

Through Federico Ronstadt's memories of his childhood we glimpse one such Sonoran episode, an insurrection led by Francisco Serna, administrator of the customs house at the coastal landing in Libertad on the Gulf of California in the Altar district. In 1875, Serna and other Sonorans became enraged by Ignacio Pesqueira's stealing of the gubernatorial election. The *sernistas* rebelled, but Pesqueira had foreseen the eventuality, had already mobilized the National Guard, and was able to triumph over his enemies in the subsequent military encounters, though not in the political ones. In 1876 the Mexican federal government was forced to intervene in the unrest and appoint an interim governor, even ordering Serna's troops to serve as auxiliaries to the federal force.[2]

Through the Ronstadt memoirs as well, we are better able to understand the sense of independence and self-reliance found even today among many lifelong residents of modern Sonora and Baja California. In the nineteenth century, diseases and injuries were commonplace, and professional medical care was next to nonexistent in the largely rural areas of the state. Recovery was an act of providence. Death, a frequent result, engendered grief tempered by a sense of resignation.

Sonorans and *Californios* typically were a people isolated from major sources of supply and remote from the centers of federal, political, military, and economic power in Mexico City or other centers of industrial production. Sonorans and residents of Baja California had to depend largely on themselves for their livelihoods. They raised crops and cattle for themselves, and they searched for minerals that could be sold elsewhere for processing and converted to cash. Ronstadt's description of the time he spent with his mother in a remote Baja California mining camp while his father left them for a year reminds his readers how different life is for most children in the United States today. What Ronstadt may have regarded in hindsight as a character-building experience might today be branded as child abuse. But such separations and hardships were commonplace on the Sonora Desert frontier.

Not all of Ronstadt's experiences were rugged or harsh. Much of the considerable charm of these memoirs derives from his accounts of how children amused themselves: playing games, making toys, putting on circuses, and getting into mischief. Through it all, too, there were schooling, both public and private, and music. Imagine an eight-year-old boy literate enough to read Alexander Dumas's *Angel Pitou* aloud in Spanish to his mother as she, confined at their Baja California mining camp, waited to give birth to her fourth child. Or imagine the impression left on a boy by the 1870s wedding of his half-sister in the Baja California coastal town of Mulege during which a local quartet sang arias from Friedrich von Flotow's opera *Martha* to the accompaniment of a piano played by a Mexican mining engineer.

Fred Ronstadt reached Tucson fewer than three years after the arrival there of the Southern Pacific Railroad, an event that more than any other shifted the orientation of southern Arizona from north and south to east and west. The railroad was the link that brought products of the booming American industrial revolution, as well as an influx of Anglo Americans, to Tucson. In that sense, he arrived just as an economic and social volcano was about to erupt. His career ultimately took advantage of the boom, and he became founder and proprietor of the largest hardware store in southern Arizona, one that did a huge business in neighboring Sonora. He recalls for us the leaner years of the end of the nineteenth century, a preamble to his later success in achieving the American dream.

It is to the retirement and subsequent hard work of Edward Frederick Ronstadt, one of Federico's sons, and to the untiring efforts of his wife Mary Catherine and their daughter Mary Theresa Carter that we owe our thanks for the preparation of these memoirs for publication. It is they who transcribed them; it was Edward, the family historian, who located and copied the historic photographs. *Borderman* is a tribute to their perseverance, to their knowledge, and to their love.

Introduction

Edward F. Ronstadt

In May of 1903, President Theodore Roosevelt looked down from the south rim of the Grand Canyon. "Leave it as it is," he said. "You cannot improve upon it. What you can do is keep it for your children and your children's children, and all who come after you."

These words might well apply to the reminiscences of Fred Ronstadt, one of the founders of the Ronstadt family of Tucson. Before his death in December of 1954, Fred Ronstadt pencilled his memoirs in cursive script on the face and backs of sheets of Ronstadt Company stationery. They detail much of his life and times in warm, straightforward prose, including his youthful activities in Sonora, Mexico and in neighboring Baja California. These memoirs are a part of our Mexican and American heritage. Except for the integration of otherwise repetitive sections, a rearrangement of the parts in chronological order and a division of the memoirs into Mexican and American halves, the occasional addition of needed punctuation, and a summarizing of a few deleted portions, his script has been left as he wrote it. Because these reminiscences were written piecemeal over a period of several years, he sometimes forgot what his previous narrative had contained.

At family gatherings, Fred Ronstadt, or Papa as we called him, used to tell us stories about his early days in Tucson, California, Sonora, and Baja California. We urged him to write these stories down on paper. During the last years of his life, from about 1944 to 1954, often while vacationing in California, he wrote many pages of the manuscript. Although he failed to commit to paper all he might have wished and the ending is abrupt, what he did accomplish fulfilled his hope of leaving his family his memoirs. In the process, he also left present and future students of history and of United States–Mexico borderlands culture a rich legacy.

Fred Ronstadt was a collector of many bits and pieces of historical memorabilia, and he asked my mother to preserve these items for future generations of historians. For many years I have worked with his papers and photographs, most of which are now deposited in Special Collections at the University of Arizona Library. Shortly after his death, some material of his father, Colonel Frederick A. Ronstadt, was placed in the archives of the Arizona Pioneers' Historical Society—now the Arizona Historical Society—in Tucson.

Grandfather Ronstadt, Frederick Augustus, was a native of Hanover, Germany, having been born there in 1816 or 1817. He received his education in mining engineering at the University of Hanover and came to the New World about 1839 or 1840, landing at Buenos Aires, Argentina and crossing the

Andes to Chile. My father told us that in 1841 grandfather was in Lima, Peru and traveled from there to San Luis Potosí, Mexico. He became a naturalized citizen of Mexico in 1843.

It is possible Frederick Augustus came to the New World to get away from the militarism sweeping over Europe in the late 1830s. In 1839 there was a new king in Hanover, the Duke of Cambridge, uncle of Queen Victoria of England. The new king abrogated the liberal constitution his predecessor had granted his subjects, bringing on vocal protests from some of the professors in the universities. My father also told us that when grandfather Ronstadt was being considered for military service in the United States, he informed the American authorities that he had received military training while in Germany. However, he spent some twenty-three years of his life in the military service of his adopted country, Mexico, becoming colonel of the National Guard of the state of Sonora and, at one time or another, military prefect of every district in Sonora. His *Acciones de Guerra* (Military Service Record) is in the archives of the Arizona Historical Society.

The first marriage of Frederick Augustus Ronstadt was to Concepción Quiroga, with whom he had four children, two boys and two girls. She died when the children were young, and he remarried in 1867 in Altar, Sonora. His new bride was Margarita Redondo, a member of a well-known and widely respected family whose forebears had arrived in northern Mexico in the first half of the eighteenth century.

Among the early arrivals in Sonora was don Francisco Xavier Redondo, who came north from the Valle de Sinaloa as a soldier in the service of Spain to the newly established Presidio of Altar in 1753. He was accompanied by soldiers whose family names continue to be prominent in southern Arizona and northern Sonora: Angulo, Elías, Moreno, Ramírez, Sotelo, and many others. Francisco Redondo must have completed his military service by the end of the eighteenth century, because in 1792 he obtained a large grant of land from the crown for the Ocuca property located half way between Altar and Santa Ana in Sonora. His brother, Santiago, was also granted a large tract of land extending from Altar northeast to Saric and Tubutama.

By the middle of the nineteenth century, the Redondos were well known in the Altar region. Margarita's father, José María, was serving as prefect of the Altar district in 1857 at the time of the infamous filibustering expedition led to Caborca, Sonora by Henry Alexander Crabb.

My father, Fred Ronstadt, was the oldest son of Frederick Augustus Ronstadt and Margarita Redondo. He was born January 30, 1868 at Las Delicias, Sonora, a hacienda that belonged to Ignacio Pesqueira, intermittent governor of Sonora. It was located just south of the community of Banámichi on the Sonora River. Frederick Augustus had just completed a period of military service and was working some of Pesqueira's mines located nearby. He was christened Federico José María, and Ignacio Pesqueira was his godfather.

In March of 1882, when Fred was fourteen years old, he and his father traveled in a mountain wagon from Magdalena, Sonora to Tucson, Arizona Territory where Fred was to learn the blacksmithing and wagon trade. As his memoirs indicate, he did so successfully. In 1890 he married Sara Levin, daughter of Alexander Levin, owner of Levin's Park and Brewery in Tucson. By this marriage he had four children: Luisa, Laura, Fred A., and Alicia. In 1902, while Sara was expecting her fifth child, she became a casualty of a scarlet fever epidemic and died at the age of thirty-two.

One of their children, Luisa, was destined to enjoy a long and successful career as an internationally known singer, Luisa Espinel. After an extensive tour of the Spanish countryside during which she lived "with people from all walks of life, learning their traditional songs and dances," she came home to the United States. Here, "she transformed herself into more than just a singer, weaving music, acting and dance into memorable vignettes that captured something of the soul of the Spanish people themselves. During the early 1930s, she toured the nation, performing in theaters and on college campuses, winning praise for musical integrity as well as her talent."[1]

In 1933 Luisa reminisced about our father for a reporter from the *Arizona Daily Star.* "There were summer evenings I remember when the moon shadows of the grape leaves latticed the arbor, and my father sitting there, his face illumined, would accompany his songs on his guitar and later tell us marvelous stories of when he was a little boy. . . . The most vivid memories of my childhood are interwoven with music and mostly the music of my father, who loved it. It was his whole life in those days; his business was a secondary consideration."[2]

Given Papa's love of music and the fact that he was founder of what probably was Tucson's first orchestra, the *Club Filarmónico Tucsonense*, it is not surprising that some of his children should have shared that love. My brother Gilbert and I continue to sing songs our father taught us. Several of Fred's grandchildren and great-grandchildren continue the tradition. Best known among them is one of Gilbert's daughters, Linda Ronstadt, who has appeared as a singer in concerts throughout the world, in movies, and on television, and who is one of today's premier recording artists.

The year after Sara's death, Lupe Dalton, daughter of Winnall A. Dalton, applied for a position at the Ronstadt Company as bookkeeper. Her father was the son of Henry Dalton and Guadalupe Zamorano. Henry Dalton, an Englishman, had arrived in California in 1845 when it was still part of Mexico. He bought land near Mission San Gabriel and became *mayordomo* (secular administrator) at the mission. He subsequently bought the Santa Anita *rancho,* land that after passing through several owners—including his son-in-law, Luis Wolfskill—was purchased in 1875 by Elias Jackson "Lucky" Baldwin. Henry Dalton's wife, Guadalupe, was the daughter of don Agustín Vicente Zamorano of Monterey, who in 1834 introduced the printing press to California.[3]

Shortly after Lupe Dalton's appearance at the Ronstadt Company, Fred Ronstadt fell in love with her and she with him. She was twenty-two years old at the time. They were married on Valentine's Day in 1904 and had four sons by their union: William, Alfred, Gilbert, and Edward. The

Ronstadt house located at 607 North Sixth Avenue in Tucson, now listed on the National Register of Historic Sites, was built by Fred that same year as a present to his new bride. The architect was Henry Trost, designer of many of Tucson's fine homes.[4]

The Ronstadt wagon and carriage factory was prospering in 1901 when it was incorporated as the F. Ronstadt Company.[5] This name continued until the 1930s when it was changed to the Ronstadt Hardware and Machinery Company, a short-lived operation that went into receivership because of poor management. Fred Ronstadt, who was sixty-five years old at the time, had been planning to retire and had made plans to sell the business to three of his associates. While he and Mrs. Ronstadt were traveling in Europe on a well-deserved vacation, his associates's mismanagement, coupled with effects of the 1929 stock market crash, practically ruined the business. When the receivership came to an end, Fred was still hoping to retire, but his son Alfred urged him to stay on, foreseeing the possibility that some of his sons might want to go into the business. Fred had sold his property on the corner of Sixth Avenue and Broadway in 1929 to Jack Martin and Dr. Meade Clyne, and with some of the money from this sale, he was able to buy the business from the receiver and bring in J. W. Briscoe who became the general manager.

In the years following 1900, the business expanded its scope of operations and carried a line of general hardware, tractors, farm implements and repair parts, road building and construction machinery and equipment, and industrial supplies. In the early 1900s Ronstadt became Tucson's first Oldsmobile dealer and later handled Studebaker, E. M. Flanders, and several other lines of automotive equipment. The automobile lines were discontinued, but the company continued to handle automotive parts and tires as well as a gasoline station where in 1929 one could buy a gallon of gasoline for seventeen cents.

In 1935 the firm incorporated under the name of F. Ronstadt Hardware Company with Fred Ronstadt serving as president, Gilbert Ronstadt as vice-president, and J. W. Briscoe as secretary treasurer and general manager. The improved economy during the New Deal and the prosperity of the World War II years helped the expansion of the business.

Fred Ronstadt continued to be active in the business up to the time of his death in 1954. J. W. Briscoe became president. In 1965 Briscoe retired and my brother Gilbert and I assumed the principal offices and management of the company. In 1983 Gilbert and I retired and our sons Eddie and Mike became the officers of the business. Over the years, many of Fred's grandchildren and even a few great-grandchildren had the opportunity and privilege of working for, learning, and contributing to the business their grandfather had founded. The F. Ronstadt Company went out of business in 1985.

Throughout his life in the twentieth century, Fred Ronstadt continued his many civic activities. He was chairman of the Water and Agricultural Committee of the Tucson Chamber of Commerce, a member of the Tucson Rotary Club, and a participant in many musical endeavors. He was among the organizers of the Tucson Symphony Orchestra, and in the mid-1920s he directed a production of Victor Herbert's *Red Mill*. He was an active member and onetime president of the Arizona Pioneers' Historical Society.

My mother, Lupe Ronstadt, died on October 10, 1974, twenty years after the death of her husband. She was ninety-two years old.

In his later years, Papa told us there was a cold spell when he and his father traveled north en route to Tucson in 1882. As they passed Calabasas, Fred's father turned to him and said: "Now you are in the United States of America, without any question the greatest country in the world. You will enjoy great liberty and protection under the American government and you must always feel and show deep affection for that. When you become a man, you may want to establish yourself in the United States. See that your life and your conduct are such as will entitle you to the privilege of American citizenship."

Papa never forgot his father's words. Sixty-seven years later, when he was 81, he wrote down these comments for a talk to his employees at the Ronstadt store: "We still know that no other country in the world can compare with ours. I say this not only because I know it, as every other American, but because of the gratitude I feel for the liberty and protection that I have enjoyed here for 67 years under the flag. I wonder how many of us fully appreciate the wonderful privilege of being a citizen of the United States?"

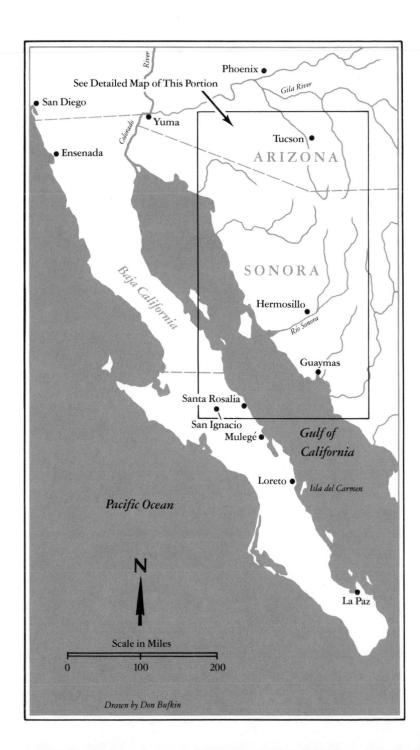

See Detailed Map of This Portion

Phoenix ●

Gila River

San Diego ●

Colorado

● Yuma

Tucson ●

● Ensenada

ARIZONA

Baja California

SONORA

Hermosillo ●

Río Sonora

Guaymas ●

Santa Rosalia ●

San Ignacio

Mulegé ●

Gulf of California

Loreto ● *Isla del Carmen*

Pacific Ocean

N

La Paz ●

Scale in Miles

0   100   200

Drawn by Don Bufkin

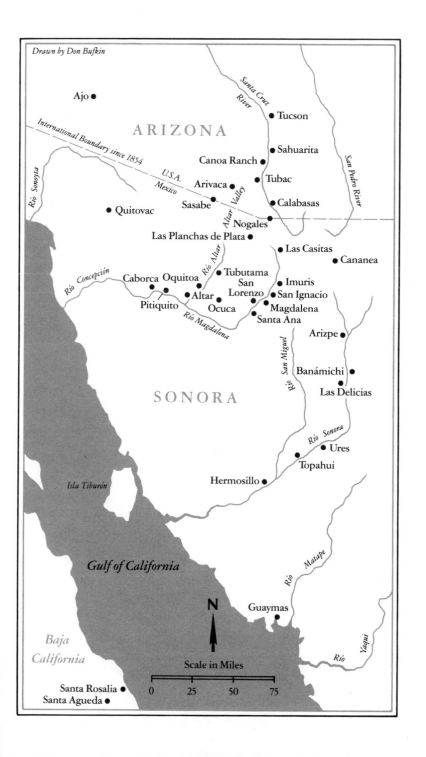

Drawn by Don Bufkin

Ajo

ARIZONA

International Boundary since 1854

U.S.A.
Mexico

Río Sonoyta

Quitovac

Santa Cruz River

Tucson

Sahuarita

Canoa Ranch

Arivaca   Tubac

Sasabe   Calabasas

Altar Valley

San Pedro River

Nogales

Las Planchas de Plata

Río Altar

Las Casitas

Cananea

Río Concepción

Caborca   Oquitoa   Tubutama

San   Imuris
Lorenzo   San Ignacio

Altar

Pitiquito   Ocuca   Magdalena

Río Magdalena   Santa Ana

Arizpe

Río San Miguel

Banámichi

Las Delicias

SONORA

Río Sonora

Ures

Topahui

Hermosillo

Isla Tiburón

Gulf of California

Río Matape

Río

N

Guaymas

Baja
California

Scale in Miles

Santa Rosalia
Santa Agueda

Río

Yaqui

0   25   50   75

Memoirs of
Federico José María Ronstadt

1

Sonora, Mexico
and
Baja California

Before I say anything about myself, I wish to note down a few things about my father and my mother. My father, Frederick Augustus Ronstadt, was born in Hanover, Germany, and educated at the university of the same city. His father's name was Godfrey Ronstadt, and as far as we knew he [Godfrey] had only one sister, named Henrietta. He came from Germany with a group of engineers to Buenos Aires, from there by muleback across the Andes to Chile and by water to San Francisco; from San Francisco overland to San Diego and Arizona & Sonora in the early fifties [1850s]. In the records of the Arizona Pioneers' Historical Society there is a paper telling of a report made by my father at that time on what was then the Ajo Mine. Mr. Sam Hughes knew about this, and he told us about this paper.

In Sonora my father found ready occupation, not only in mining work but in managing the large haciendas for some of the leading men of that state at that time. He took charge of General [Manuel] Gándara's Hacienda de Topahui between Ures and Hermosillo and here he built a cotton and wool mill, a flour mill, and tannery &

made cotton & wool fabrics, leather, soap, candles, sugar, flour & other food products; also lumber and iron things needed were all made there by native labor from raw materials produced in the same place. He made many friends, and when the country needed trained soldiers he was given command of Mexican troops to fight Indians and revolutionists. He served as an officer in the Mexican army during the French invasion when Maximilian tried to establish his empire [1864–1867] and also during the 3 years' War of the Reforma [1858–1860].

When General [Ignacio] Pesqueira, then Governor of Sonora, General García Morales and their staffs had to change the state capital from Ures to Tubac on account of the Maximilian supporters [1865–1866], my father came with them and happened to be the only one of the entire party who escaped the malaria that attacked all of them soon after they arrived at Tubac. He had to take charge and doctor the sick with large doses of quinine until they could help themselves. It was here that Governor Pesqueira commissioned my father to negotiate a loan from the people of Tucson, pledging the revenue of the state of Sonora and his own personal wealth as security. My father obtained some $24,000.00 from Sam Hughes, Tully & Ochoa, Hiram Stevens and other Tucson citizens. Firearms, ammunition, provisions and other materials were purchased to equip a troop of Mexican volunteers, and with these as a nucleus they incorporated more as they marched to Hermosillo where Maximilian sympathizers were in control. The morning of May the 4th they attacked the city from the Cerro de las Campanas and drove the traitors out of Hermosillo and soon after from the entire state.[1]

The Governor appointed my father State Treasurer and Tax Commissioner with power to collect revenues and pay off the various loans due the citizens of Tucson. After that my father served the State of Sonora as Prefect and Military Commander of every district in Sonora at different times, the last time during the revolution of General [Francisco] Serna in 1874 when he was transferred from the Altar District to Guaymas. By this time he had given 22 years of service to the Mexican Government, much of this during periods when the soldiers had to procure their own living as best they could, and he decided to retire to private life. He accepted the management of a group of copper mines in the southern part of Lower California belonging to Mueller & Co which several years later were sold to the French Co. known as Sta. [Santa] Rosalía–El Boleo.

From Sta. Rosalía my father took a prospecting expedition over the entire peninsula to Ensenada near San Diego. He returned to La Paz and later to Sonora. His last years he was *Perito de Minas* (Mining Inspector) & mining advisor for the District of Magdalena and also helped the Sta. Fe R.R. to secure the right of way through northern Sonora when the road was built from Guaymas to Nogales & Benson [1880–1882]. He took care of claims against the R.R. until his health broke down entirely about 1886. By that time I had started a carriage shop of my own in Tucson and had my father, mother, brothers & sisters come here to make a home for me.

My father died and was buried here in 1889 [see pages 123–25]. He told me many interesting episodes of his active life but he never wrote anything. The Mexican government owed him a small fortune for his service in the army as captain & colonel during the Maximilian war & others but he never made any special effort to collect the claim.

We have in some of his records: his certificates of commissions, and his "*hoja de servicios*" (record of service) in the army.

My mother's name was Margarita Redondo. Her great grandfather, Don Francisco Redondo, came from Spain and settled the Hacienda del Ocuca about 30 miles southeast of Altar. We have a record of his work while he developed his homestead and raised a large family. They had to produce all the principal needs of life like all the old pioneers. They had their private school, a chapel where they gathered for prayer at morning and night, including the servants, and *torreones* (adobe circular two-story forts) from where they could defend their places against the Apache Indians, very numerous & ferocious in those days.

The Ocuca is still one of the best ranches in Sonora, with wonderful mesquite forests, rich valleys, running water from its own warm spring sufficient to irrigate hundreds of acres of bottom lands. Its area has been reduced by dividing much of the original land now held by various new owners.

My mother's father, Don José María Redondo, was a successful gentleman farmer, stockman, and merchant. He happened to be Prefecto of the District of Altar when the filibustering expedition of [Henry Alexander] Crabb invaded Caborca [in 1857].[2] He had a reputation for extreme kindness & patience. My mother's mother, Doña Jesús Vásquez, died during the cholera epidemic in 1848 when my mother was only 2 years old.

My grandfather Redondo died in 1879 at the very advanced age of 92. His brothers and cousins were many. Some located in Yuma, Ariz. The Martins and Rebeils of Tucson are descendants of these Redondos on their mother's side.

I was born at "*Las Delicias*," the hacienda and home of Gen. Pesqueira near Cananea in 1868 when my father was working the original Cananea mine of that time. I can remember when I must have been between 2 & 3 years old an assay room that my father had across the street from where we lived at a mining town called Banámichi not far from Cananea. I filled my cap with flakes of silver from a mound on the floor one day and ran with it across the street for home. I don't remember any more but it is almost sure that my disciplining must have started from that day.

On account of my father's mining work we never lived long in one place. About 1872 my father was working Las Planchas de Plata mine near Nogales and we lived in Magdalena.

There is where I went to school the first time. My teacher was a hunchback. I do not recall any more about him only that he gave me a *silibario,* a sort of kindergarten first reader with the alphabet and a few short words to spell. The size of the little book was about 2 1/2 x 5 inches bound in paper. I was there only a short time. After that I was sent to a larger school [all private]. The teacher, a Sr. Torres, was very severe.

My first day he punished all the boys, and this frightened me so that I crawled under my table and would not come out until one of the boys coaxed me out. I remember a few incidents of our residence in Magdalena at that time.

One day I saw some masons building an adobe wall and boys carrying the mud to them in buckets. One of the men asked me if I wanted to work (I was 4 years old). I agreed to do so and in a few minutes I reported for duty with one of my mother's copper kettles that I took from the kitchen.

Every day after the noon hour we had to take the dreaded siesta. Most of the time I would sneak out to play with neighboring boys. I remember when they had a feast during Noche Buena [Christmas] and a boy fell from the church tower while they were ringing the bells. I never see the old mission at Magdalena but what I remember this incident. I can see the boy sitting on the sill of the upper tower window on the south side, his legs hanging out over the wall, and suddenly slipping off.

Our next residence was a farm home near Pitiquito. This was the property of my mother and not far from one of my grandfather's haciendas, *"La Muralla."* The name of our farm home here was *Las Margaritas*. The old house can still be seen from the Pitiquito side of the river. They now call it *"La Casa Blanca"* and it is owned by an Amarante Martínez. At this place my father gave me a black colt which, of course, I was not big enough to ride.

One Sunday while my father had gone to some mine in the family spring wagon, my mother, my two half sisters, their grandmother who made her home with us, and a maid decided to visit my grandfather's home at Altar only 10 miles away and make the trip in one of the ox carts driven by a Yaqui stable boy who worked for us. It was fun to go and have dinner at grandfather's, but on the return trip a summer thunder storm overtook us on the road. The oxen could hardly pull the heavy cart over the soft ground full of water. I remember the prayers of the old lady with us and the fright at the flashes of lightning & thunder in the darkness. About half way the *mayordomo* [overseer] from our farm, a man named Daniel, met us with my father's saddle horse, a fine gentle gray, and my black colt newly broken to the saddle. My two half sisters rode the gray and Daniel placed my mother on the black colt and he mounted back of the saddle to hold her and guide the horse. Doña Andrea, the old grandmother, the maid, with my brother Dick, a baby, and sister Emilia and myself stayed in the ox cart with the young Indian driver. After this we felt more secure, and I don't remember how we got home, but I heard my mother say that my black colt bolted and ran through the brush for a good distance before Daniel could control him and she escaped the tree branches with a lot of bad scratches.

From this farm we moved to Altar. There I attended three different schools in a period of two years.

Here they had an epidemic of scarlet fever that killed many children. My little sister died from it. Dick was very bad, and I was not expected to live. Two boys, sons of uncle Don Luis Redondo, died at that time. They made brick vaults for their bodies and provided a receptacle for mine. Many times I was shown my *bobeda* [receptacle] after I recovered when visiting the graveyard.

The first school I attended this time was the private one of my mother's aunt, Doña María Antonia de Pompa. She had a tutor for her five boys, Miguel, Joaquín, Luis, Ernesto and Abram. The tutor's name was Don Pablo Gallardo. He was a small man and they called him Don Pablito. I remember him when he called at our home. He had a good voice and played the guitar. I still remember one of his songs, a beautiful melody to the story of a boy exiled from his own country and anxious for a home in a foreign land.

The second school was conducted by a different type, a Don Félix Rodríguez, extremely severe and autocratic. One day he came back to the school room from a horse race and found all the boys jumping and cheering for the winning horse announced by someone passing by the school. The boys were paralyzed as Don Félix walked in the school room. He made us all line up and went over the entire line with his rawhide switch and no one escaped two or three good sharp swats on the back.

The 3rd school was also a private one conducted by a Don Enrique who had a rubber foot. By that time I was 6 years old and could join the older boys in their games and devilment.

I remember two things very clearly of this period. My mother left her trunk open one day and looking for candy which she usually kept in this trunk, I found in a little box a pile of gold coins. I did not know the value of them. They were *onzas*, $16.00 pieces. I took one and went out on the street to try to buy something. I tried to buy a pocket knife at the store of Don Evaristo Araiza (he is still living at Altar nearly a 100 years old). He immediately sent word to my home that I had a $16.00 gold piece, but by the time they found me I had bought a watermelon with it from a 19 year old boy nicknamed Chichipichi who was sacristan for Father Suastegui, the town parish priest.

I was questioned at home and a messenger sent to Father Suastegui's home and the gold piece recovered. I knew I had committed a crime. I was given a good sermon and a better switching, and Don Enrique was instructed to keep me confined in school for two weeks. At recess hours I was made to sit inside of the school room fire place and a screen was placed over it so I would be concealed. At night I slept in the teacher's room. My meals were brought to me from home. I did not serve my full two weeks. I had been sitting on a rawhide chair one afternoon and for nothing better to do I would reach under to break slivers from the chair frame to chew them, with one of the slivers came a red ant and stung me in the end of the tongue.

This trouble was not enough to get me liberty but a few days later Doctor Harvey, an English doctor friend of my father who had a room with us at home, brought a gray horse that looked like my father's gentle gray. Brother Dick mistook him for the gray that he knew, attempted to play with him and got a kick that broke his right arm near the shoulder. This accident softened my mother's heart and I was brought home from my school jail.

We lived at a house owned by Don Pedro Zepeda right across the street from Don José M. Salazar. His two boys, José Jr., older than I, and Rodolfo, about my age, were my playmates. Rodolfo and I would frequently fight.

One day we were clinched in the middle of the street pulling each other's hair with all our might. My father pulled me away and gave me a whipping. After that Rodolfo and I were more careful as he had a similar experience after our hair pulling match.

One birthday we had a party at home and several of the guests present gave me dimes for singing a little comic song that I knew.

> *A la noche voy a verte*
> *Escondido del tió*
> *Dime se estaras despierta*
> *Para cuando te haga 'phish.'*[3]

After this a whistling strain, etc.

While the party was going on I went across the street, bought firecrackers with all the dimes I had, invited Rodolfo to a back lot, and we had a celebration.

A party of Americans stopped a few days at our house. They had mining business with my father. There were no hotels there, so they were invited to visit with us. One of them, a young man not very tall, used to amuse me by turning somersaults and walking on his hands. He was a fine athlete, and we boys used to admire him immensely.

About this time the Serna revolution, started at Pitiquito, was in full swing. My father was in charge of the District of Guaymas, and we were waiting to go to Guaymas when the government troops and the Serna revolutionists had their first battle two miles south of Altar in Los Puertecitos. We had seen the Sernistas well mounted, three or four hundred strong, ride out of Altar to meet Col. [Francisco] Altamirano's Red Shirts. The civilian men in Altar were conspicuous by their absence so we only had women and children and a few old men. The boys large enough to be out were all on the house roofs trying to get a glimpse of the battle.

We did not have long to wait. First we heard the shooting and next the Sernistas running their horses for dear life through the town in the direction of Tucson. Next the Red Shirts of Col. Altamirano shouting *Viva Pesqueira! Muera Serna!* [Death to Serna!].[4] The next thing was sacking [of] the closed stores by the soldiers. One of the officers happened to be a friend of my father and came to our home for living quarters. His son, a lieutenant, had been shot in his right arm. He also stayed at our home for several days.

On account of all the stores being closed for several weeks the homes had been out of sugar, coffee and other staples. After a family consultation my mother bought a sack of coffee and some sugar from the sacking Red Shirt soldiers.

The next thing I remember is a spring wagon taking us to Guaymas. After several days of travel we arrived at Guaymas. My father had a house ready for us located a few blocks from the bay.

I was anxious to see the sea and climbed to the roof at daylight the following morning expecting a great thrill. I could only see the clear blue sky in the horizon and the same clear blue of the mirror-like bay. I was clearly disappointed, not being sure that there was any sea near us. My father took me over to the edge of the water after breakfast. I made sure that the water was salty by tasting it.

At Guaymas I was sent to what was then considered to be the best school in Sonora, a private school conducted by Prof. Leocadio

Salcedo, a native of Peru who had been in Sonora for several years educating many young sons and daughters of the leading families of Sonora and Sinaloa. I was 7 years old then. Prof. Salcedo was a friend of my father and made me feel at home. Here I started to take English. The method was Carrenos Ollendorf.

José M. Maytorena, who was Governor of Sonora during [Francisco] Madero's administration [as President of Mexico, 1911–13] was my schoolmate and chum. His home was a few doors from ours in the same block. In the garden they had a fence made of steel rods about 5/16" and about the right length to make a sword by looping one end for a handle. We stole a good many rods from the Maytorena garden fence to arm boys of our party. We had a boys' revolution. Our gang was Pesquerista and the opposing gang Sernista. I remember being captured one night and placed in "*cepo de campana.*" This was tying one on a pole across and under the knees and elbows so it was impossible to move.

Another time a vicious dog was turned on us and I happened to be the victim. The dog was a large black one and he threw me on my face and chewed my back before they could drive him off.

General Pesqueira had left his younger brother Pepe [José J. Pesqueira] as acting governor against the wishes of many of his friends. Pepe Pesqueira was known to be incompetent for the place. He sent a troop of mounted Red Shirts under a captain with a letter to my father asking him to arrest 18 or 20 of the leading citizens of Guaymas including Prof. Salcedo and several personal friends of my father, claiming that they were Serna sympathizers. My father refused to comply with the request and sent a reply to Pepe Pesqueira stating that since he had not sent him an official order for this arrest but only a private letter requesting that it should appear as a voluntary act on the part of the Prefect of the District (my father), he was not duty bound and furthermore considered the idea preposterous and extremely unfair and dangerous for the Pesqueira party. He also sent his resignation.

A few weeks later the same captain came back with 20 mounted soldiers and an order for my father to turn over his office to Don Plutarco Elías. Don Plutarco Elías was the father of the present Mexican ex-president Plutarco Elías Calles [1923–28]. Don Plutarco became *prefecto* of Guaymas on my father's resignation. He immediately ordered the arrest of 18 or 20 of Guaymas's leading citizens. They were confined in the rooms of the *prefectura* adjoining our home. In the meantime my father had accepted the management of the copper mine, "*La Ley,*" owned by Mueller & Co. and sailed for Sta. Rosalía, Lower California. The ladies of Guaymas appealed to Col. [José María] Rangel who was commanding the 15th Battalion of Federals at Guaymas. Col. Rangel decided it was time for the Federal Army to take charge, and with a troop of Federal soldiers formed in front of the *prefectura,* he demanded the surrender of the prisoners to his care. Don Plutarco could do nothing else but comply, and the men were saved. This incident, when reported to the President of Mexico, caused him to declare the State of Sonora under federal control, and sent General [Vicente] Mariscal to take charge of the situation. This ended the Serna-Pesqueira revolution in Sonora. Mariscal remained in charge until Porfirio Díaz was made President [in 1876].

Soon after my father arrived at Lower California he arranged for us to sail from Guaymas. We took passage in a two-masted Mexican schooner named the *Rambler.* For 24 hours we had a dead calm and could see the lights of Guaymas from just outside of the bay. The third day in the evening a hard *noroeste* [northwesterly storm] came. There were no cabins on this boat. We were all on deck and the captain tied some heavy canvas over us to guard us against heavy seas washing over the deck.

Next morning we were anchored at Mulege across the Gulf. From there to Sta. Rosalía was a short sail along the Lower California coast. My father was there waiting for us. We had a meal of dates and goat's milk at the Company's warehouse, the only building there.

My mother & the two children, Dick & Emily, remained here while my father rode his saddle mule to the mine 10 miles away to get mules for us all. He took me along riding behind him and tied to his waist with a scarf. The country here is mountainous and the only roads were mule trails. We passed two or three mines, the *Cerro Verde,* the *Purgatorio,* and the *Limbo* which later was acquired by my father. Before getting to "*La Ley*" mine we had to go through a very narrow passage in the mountains called La Angostura. The sides were almost perpendicular of smooth gray granite and the box not over six feet wide in places. *La Ley* had only one building made of rough lumber. This contained the Company's store and my father's office and assay room. The warehouses were tunnels blasted on the side of the mountain. The mess room was also in a tunnel and the houses of the miners were all of stones, piled up, and brush. Some had thatched roofs made of tule, brought from Santa Agueda, a village 9 miles away. The water had to be brought in 10 gal. kegs from a well 6 miles toward the sea on mules & burros. They had a regular *chinchorro* (a herd of 20 or 30 pack mules and burros with leather *aparejos* [pack saddles]) making a daily trip for water. The ore was all handled by hand, with wheel barrows running in and out of tunnels by men, like an army of human ants. The water was brackish & with a taste of copper, difficult to drink. My mother had to boil it and filter it through ollas.

The same boat that brought us from Guaymas had also brought the lumber for the house in which we were to live and also an American carpenter named John Campbell.

Our first day at this mine we had to camp in a brush cabin that my father had had cleaned for us. He ordered the meals be brought over to us from the mess house in the tunnel. The first meal, however, never reached us. My father overheard the cook telling one of the miners (while he was carrying a large box with our dinner) that the family of the new superintendent were too high toned to come to his mess room. My father said something about this to the cook when he handed the box to us. The cook made some disagreeable remark to my father, and my father kicked him out of the place and threw his box containing our dinner after him. That day we had no dinner.

My mother begged my father to let her cook over a place made of a few rocks, so we got some utensils from the store and got along fine for several days while they were building our house.

It was discovered that the lumber was not enough to roof and floor the two large rooms that were up. My mother told my father that she preferred floors and for a roof we had heavy white canvas until the next boat brought some more lumber. For a kitchen and pantry we had a large tunnel. A shed or porch connected these tunnels with the house.

The poor cook who had trouble with my father was killed with a rock over the side of his head in a quarrel with a miner only a few weeks after we came to the mine. The miners were principally

Yaquis. The provisions were corn, beans, dry meat, lard, sugar, coffee, and dry fruits like dates, figs, raisins, also potatoes, rice, onions, garlic, chili, macaroni, cheese, no milk or butter and very little wheat flour. In season we would get fresh fruits and vegetables from Santa Agueda.

The copper ore was cleaned and sampled carefully. Only that which assayed 40% could be used. After all the hand cleaning and sacking it was taken by mules and burros to the sea coast. The sacks were emptied and the ore piled up until there was enough for a ship load. Sailing barks would come from England around Cape Horn, and would anchor a mile or more from shore. The ore was again sacked, taken aboard the ship in lighters by oarsmen, hoisted on deck and the sacks again emptied into the ship's hold. This would be taken back to be smelted in England.

The arrival of these English barks was a gala day, as they would bring supplies from Europe. I remember one time when my father bought a case of eggs from some sea bird. My mother would use them only for baking. Also several crocks of a yellow butter that most of the time was melted. The only person that would eat this butter was the carpenter John Campbell. He would use it in his coffee as cream.

Our first summer at the mine was found unbearable, and my father took us to Santa Agueda where we had a good adobe house that belonged to one of the wealthy ranchers there, Don Anastacio Villavicencio. They had stored their furniture in one of the rooms and we had all the rest of the house for ourselves. The Villavicencio family were then living at their cattle ranch some distance away. This old house was built at the foot of a hill the top of which was full of pitahayas, a delicious cactus pear the size of an apple. In front we had a valley with several acres covered with a jungle of *carrizo* [cane] and a stream of crystal water running through it.

The village or town was across a creek about a mile away. This little river had running water all the time. The bed of it was really nearly all solid granite. In some places the sides were flat slabs of granite and had water holes deep enough to swim and dive.

One day while wading in this creek I stepped into a hole beyond my depth and would have drowned if an older and larger boy had not come to my rescue. I remember that I would kick the bottom and bob my head out of the water to cough the water out of my lungs and shout. I did this several times. Evidently the bottom was only a few inches beyond my height. I was about 8 years old at that time.

My father would come to spend Sundays with us, and it was then that he told me the tale of "Ali Baba and the Forty Thieves." I read *"Angel Pitou"* by Dumas to my mother while she was confined when her fourth baby was born at this place. I never forgot the impression this book made on me. I have tried to find it to read it again but never succeeded.

We had a lot of chickens here and many were killed by wildcats. These cats would go into our kitchen at night if the door was left open and steal food.

In Lower California at the time everybody had a large knife, and the boys would carry them as soon as they could get them. I had one with me all the time. I cut a tunnel several feet deep through the carrizo jungle and at the end made a sort of room where we would play. My brother Dick was 5 years old by that time.

We also found an old tunnel in the side of the hill back of the house with a chest of rusty tools. At another time we broke into the rooms where the owners of the house had their furniture stored and found some two or three silver dimes on the floor. We explored for more treasure several times when my mother was not around but never found any more.

We certainly enjoyed our stay in Santa Agueda. We had our own pool of crystal water in a cabin cut out of the carrizo jungle. Here we would play and started to learn to swim. The cook left us, and my mother happened to be in bed with a bad cold and fever. I had to do the cooking under her instructions until my father came from the mine at the end of the week and hired another cook.

When we left Santa Agueda my father had resigned as Supt. of *"La Ley"* and acquired the *"El Limbo"* mine to work it for himself. Here we found that he had built a good house with 3 large rooms and a porch. He made the walls of stone laid in mud. The roof was thatch of tule and the floors petate mats.

When we started from Santa Agueda we had our furniture loaded on pack mules. The table with its four legs sticking up was all broken up when the mule got scared and ran with it under some of the branches.

At the Limbo Mine we lived through the winter months of 1877. My father had his assay office in the house and I used to help him to do the grinding. I also knew how to clean ore and would gather the good pieces that the miners would throw over the dump until I had a ton of clean ore. My father would give me sacks and pay me twelve pesos for it.

I had a small saddle mule and would ride with my father to the other mines. A German named Pablo Dato who wore side whiskers was running *La Providencia, Bon Plan,* and *Cerro Verde,* all within 6 to 8 miles from our mine. A German company was working a marble quarry on the coast. The manager's name was Carlos Eisman. All the Germans would visit my father often and had good times. Most of their conversation, however, was in German and we could not understand it.

My father was the justice of the peace, "*juez local,*" for the group of mines and every week the mine policeman, a very tall man named Justo Chávez, would bring someone for trial. I only remember one murder. A boy about 19 who worked for us stoned a man to death from fear that this man would kill him. It was a sad affair, not so much on account of the dead man, as he was a bully who had killed several people, but because of the poor boy who had to be sent to Mulege for trial accused of murder. Mulege was the county seat (*cabecera de distrito*).

We were sent to Mulege to attend school the summer of 1878. My mother sent me to inquire about this boy and I found him in a tunnel cut out of the granite. He was locked in there, with the same clothes he had on when he killed the man, and was half starved. My mother sent him some of father's old clothes and several times she would send me with food for him.

The house where we lived in Mulege, while located in one of the main streets, had its back yard facing the Estero, a river that ran along one side of the town to the sea. Our next door neighbor had a large canoe, which he used for fishing, tied to his back porch. We had a dandy swimming hole in our back yard surrounded on three sides by a heavy growth of tule.

At Mulege I attended a private school conducted by Don Jesús Padilla assisted by his son Ismael and his oldest daughter Erlinda. Brother Dick was now about six years old and had to go to school.

He had to be carried by myself and another boy by force as if going to jail.

We soon became acquainted with many of the Mulege families. The Prefecto, Don Pablo Poza, acted as godfather when our baby brother Joe was baptized.

Mulege had date palm groves and large groves of olives, particularly across the river. For 6/4 cents (a *medio*) we could get a large soup plate full and piled high with delicious olives pickled in brine. Dates and other fruits were also very cheap.

Of our stay in Mulege some episodes remain clear in my mind. The first happened to me on a Sunday when I crossed to the other side of the river over a narrow foot bridge at the lower end of the town to see the date palm groves. I walked through these groves towards the sea for a mile or more. I had gathered a small basket full of dates as I went along. The tide had gone down in the late afternoon; and as it appeared to me that the water in the river was only a few inches deep, I decided to wade across it to the other side where I could see the road from the port to the town and better walking than returning to the bridge a mile away through the heavy growth. I took off my shoes, rolled up my trousers and started across. For a hundred yards or so the water was only to my knees, but all of a sudden I stepped into the channel, deeper than my height. Fortunately, this channel was not very wide and I soon reached the other side where I could walk on the bottom with my head out of the water. My shoes were safely tied to my belt but the basket of dates was gone. It was not yet dark when I had to walk through the town to reach home, while most of the neighbors were sitting outside. My humiliation may be surmised.

The next thing was when I went to the port to meet my father who was coming from the mine on a sailing schooner that had weathered a storm and came into port with both masts broken off and all the rigging banged up on deck. Hearing my father tell about how they expected to be lost all through the night with the ship out of control in the storm made a never to be forgotten impression on me.

At another time one of the Mexía boys who had fishing boats invited me to a night of fishing with a large net. We pulled out a boat full of fish about two o'clock in the morning and many strange sea animals, one that they called *guitarra* [guitar] on account of its shape that would give us an electric shock if touched with our bare feet.

My half sister Chonita was married at Mulege to Carmelo Mexía, a member of one of the leading families of the town. I remember the wedding feast and that a mining engineer, who was married to one of the Mexía girls, Don Manuel Tinoco, was a good pianist. He had organized a quartet that sang parts of the opera *Martha* that day.

Soon after Chonita's wedding we returned to my father's mine. He had failed to find ore of the required 40% in sufficient quantities to make it pay and had to discontinue operations.

Before we left Mulege I had a chance to see how the pearl fishers handled the business at the time. The Fierro family had several small ships engaged in this industry. They would claim a portion of sea water and land along the coast in the same manner that a gold claim was filed on land for their exclusive exploitation. They had divers with diving suits. The shells taken out by these divers would all be sent to Mulege to be opened later for pearls, but they also had a number of men who dived in shallow water with only a stout knife and took out three or four shells at every dive, whatever they could find and take in their hands. These fellows would dive in water 20 feet deep and deeper. At the end of the day their little mound of shells would be divided, half of them for the diver, and half for the owner of the field or camp. These shells would be opened on the spot. The divers' shells would sometimes have valuable pearls which they would sell to the camp owner or take with them to the towns for a better price. Many of these poor fellows would be attacked by sharks and sometimes killed.

The Lower California gulf coast has produced fine pearls from the time of the conquistadors to the present day.

When we returned to the mine "*El Limbo*" we again had no school and my time was taken in helping my father in the assay office and walking over the hills. Sometimes I would ride my father's saddle mule or one of my own burros. I had two, one gray and one brown. The brown one was the best one, a pacer and very easy to ride. On account of the roughness of the country, horses were used very little. I would amuse myself also by digging tunnels on the hillside and building stone parapets (*trincheras*) as those used by the Indians.

When the work in the mine was stopped, my father took four of his best men and ten or twelve good mules for riding and for carrying equipment and supplies and started on a prospecting expedition going north over trails all the way to Ensenada near San Diego. This trip took him nearly a whole year. He took along a quantity of dry dates for mule fodder. These were free for the gathering at the town of San Ignacio where date palms grow wild in such profusion that they have to be thinned down to get the fruit.

The family remained at the mine while my father took this trip and we did not hear from him for many months until he reached the mine *El Real del Castillo* near Ensenada. His first letter to my mother told about how they traveled over mountains where they had to build their own trails as they went along and would take weeks to make a 100 miles without any sign of water. They had to carry water on mule backs for the men and the mules.

I never forget the feeling of desolation we had at home the evening we saw my father and his party ride away from the mine. We retired early after saying our evening prayers with heavy hearts. Before I fell asleep I heard the steps of my father's saddle mule coming towards the house. He had forgotten his compass and had to come back after it.

My mother had a young Yaqui servant to do the outside work, cut firewood for us, look after the pack burros that we had for hauling water from a well four miles away and do other chores. An old Mexican woman, Doña Reyes, who had kept a boarding place for the miners while the mine was active, was the only person remaining at the mine near us. She had a boy about 7 years old and two daughters, Cuca, about 12 years, and Bersabe, about 10. These girls would help my mother with the housework. Doña Reyes continued to run an eating place for men from "*Cerro Verde,*" a neighboring mine about three miles away.

My mother had some cash for living expenses. We would get provisions from the store of *La Providencia* about nine miles away on the other side of the mountain. I would always go along with Juan, the Yaqui boy, and help him draw the water, fill the 10 gallon barrels with a funnel, cut wood and also bring "*dipna,*" a very good feed for mules and cattle, growing all over the hills in that country.

It is a green tree similar to our palo verde excepting that the branches grow thin and straight like broom corn. It is very succulent and sweet. The stock eat even the bark of these trees and get fat on it.

About twice a month we would ride to Santa Agueda, nine miles over the mts., to get fresh vegetables and fruit such as we could get. One day I made this trip alone when Juan was away and on my return I told my mother that I could also get the water by helping the water men who also came from the other mines to get their water from the same well. I tried it the first time without Juan. While the water men would draw the water with a hand windlass in 10 gallon buckets from the 100 foot open well and fill the water troughs, I would fill their 10 gallon barrels, sometimes 50 or more, with a can and funnel to get 20 gallons of water to fill my own.

They would help me load my two 10 gallon kegs on my burro and the rest was easy. I only had to drive my pack burro and ride the other one home.

Unloading the water at home was easy. One of the girls would hold one of the 10 gallon kegs on the right side of the *aparejo* (pack saddle), partly held by the X rope while I would let the left side keg slide down to the ground. I also tried bringing a burro load of firewood and my mother and I decided that Juan was not needed, particularly as he had been going away to visit friends at the other mines and staying away for one or two days at a time.

From that time on I was a person of responsibilities. I had to keep up the water supply, and the firewood, and look after the burros. Sometimes I would hobble them and let them range in the hills until I found that they would never go far from the house. Then I would let them loose without hobbles. I learned to track them when I wanted to bring them home. Sometimes I would lose the tracks and have to walk for hours before finding them. However, this was less work than to have to bring a load of *dipna* for them every day to keep them in the corral.

We had a lot of English Red chickens of the fighting breed. A friend of ours loaned us a very fine thoroughbred rooster. We kept it for some time and when my mother thought we should return it she sent me with it and a note of thanks. The owner of this rooster lived about ten miles away from us. I was given the directions for reaching this mine. I had to climb to the top of the mountain to the west of us, travel south along the top for a few miles until the trail would go down the canyon on the other side and then a short distance up this canyon where this mine was supposed to be. I saddled one of my burros, took the rooster in my left arm, and started on my journey. I followed the trail along the top of this mountain until it started to get dark. I could not find the trail going down to the bottom of the canyon on the west so I decided to go down anyway, thinking that I would find the trail on the bottom. I started my burro down the side and I finally reached the bottom, part of the time crawling and sometimes sliding. The mountain burros in that part of the country are almost like goats to negotiate the rocks. I traveled along the bottom of the canyon for some distance without finding any trail or signs of travel until it was so dark I could not see the ground. I realized the futility of going farther and decided to return. By that time the rooster that must have actually weighed 4 or 5 pounds felt like half a ton on my arm. I tried to find a place on the side of the canyon where my burro could climb back to the trail I had left on top, but the more I looked the steeper and rougher the side of the mountain appeared. I could only continue going down along the bottom which, for my good fortune, happened to be easy to travel. After many hours I came to the sea shore and the well-traveled road to *Sta. María,* another mine that I knew. I was then about 15 miles from our mine, but I knew how to reach home.

I had to travel east along the coast until I could turn the point of the mountain and then turn south along the other canyon where our mine was about eight miles from the coast.

I must have arrived home just before dawn. My poor mother had sent Doña Reyes' boy to "*Cerro Verde*" to get two men to send them to look for me. Fortunately, they had not started when I came home with my burro pretty well tired out and my left arm nearly paralyzed from holding the rooster.

My mother had another bad scare when I failed to return one evening. This time she knew I had gone only a short distance to get one of the burros and she walked with brother Dick (7 years old) along the trail and met me lying on the bareback of the burro walking towards the house. I only remember that while riding the burro bareback it stumbled and I fell hitting a rock with my left hip. I must have found the burro near me when I got up and climbed on its back. I was lame for a long time from this fall.

Another time, returning from Santa Agueda where I had been sent for vegetables, I had Dick riding with me on one of the burros. We started from Santa Agueda in the middle of the afternoon, expecting to get home before dark, but our burro got sick and refused to go when we were about half way. I tried to make it walk ahead of us, tried to lead it also, but she would not budge. She laid down groaning and I had to take the saddle off and leave the burro there thinking it was going to die. I carried the saddle on my back and led Dick by the hand over the trail which I could hardly see. Poor Dick was scared and crying all the way.

We got home about midnight. Next morning I borrowed the

mule from Don Justo Chávez, the policeman, who happened to be at our mine that morning. I went back to see what had happened to my burro. I only found a wet spot and the signs where coyotes had taken what must have been a prematurely born burro baby. The mother went back to Sta. Agueda and we brought her back a few weeks later.

Doña Reyes knew that my mother had a few dollars in the house and persuaded her to make small loans to some of the *Cerro Verde* miners who were boarding at her place. The rates were one bit (12 1/2 cents) on the dollar per week. That was the prevailing rate and it was not long before my mother was making money. Doña Reyes would make the loans and collect the interest and principle on paydays for my mother. Doña Reyes probably collected commissions also because her eating house business prospered. Unbeknown to my mother she was also selling liquor. My mother discovered this one day when in a free for all fight at *Cerro Verde* one of Doña Reyes' boarders was seriously stabbed and Doña Reyes and her children came running to our house begging my mother to let them hide a few bottles of mescal, fearing that the judge from *Cerro Verde* might trace the liquor to her house and have it searched. The sale of liquor was prohibited in all the mines of that district. She told my mother with tears in her eyes: "Please let me hide these bottles in your kitchen. They would never think of coming here for them and if they find them at my home they will ruin me." My mother took pity on her, but that was the end of Doña Reyes' liquor business. She told us that from a quart of mescal that cost her $1.00 she would serve 20 drinks at a quarter each.

One 24th of June, San Juan's Day, I was sent to Santa Agueda after vegetables. San Juan is celebrated by the Mexicans and Yaquis and at Santa Agueda on that day a lot of miners had gathered to have a good time, principally by drinking mescal. About 3 P.M. the hilarity was at fever heat and quarrels were starting. I was standing by the side of a young man getting ready to start for home when a shot rang out and the fellow at my side doubled up pressing his hands against his stomach. The bullet had plowed across his stomach missing his intestines by a half inch. This was the signal for a general riot. Don Justo Chávez, the policeman, was on hand and mounted on his mule charged the crowd single handed, firing his pistol now and then. I did not stay to see the end. This time I was riding a good mule and I took to the road at a gallop.

I thought the Yaquis would cut Don Justo to pieces, as they all had knives, but in some way his mule brought him out of the mob unhurt. On the road home I saw one man lying by the side of the road moaning and cursing. We heard later that this man had had his stomach slashed and died. Several others were cut badly.

My trips to Sta. Agueda were many. I used to walk sometimes following a short cut over the mountain. One time I became so thirsty I could not hold enough water to quench my thirst when I finally reached the water creek near Sta. Agueda. I am sure that, if I ever go to that country, I can locate all my old landmarks. Near our mine, *El Limbo,* was an overhanging ledge perhaps a 100 feet high like a leaning wall along a dry sandy wash. We used to talk to it and get a perfect response back from the echo. We called this wall *El Cantil* [The Steep Rock].

The miners and ranchers of Lower California would tell us tales of ghosts and witches that could take the form of cats and talk, and tell these stories so sincerely that it was difficult for us to doubt their veracity. They believed them themselves. They also told us of haunted mines where the spirits of miners killed in them would come out after dark. I used to pass an abandoned mine when going after water. One night I imagined I could hear the steps following me and started to run. The faster I ran the louder the steps following me. I surely had a bad scare.

My mother was called to Mulege while our half sister Chonita was ill. The wife of Don Justo Chávez was left with Dick and me at home to take care of us. My little sister Emilia and the baby Joe went with my mother. From time to time I would go to the beach hoping to see some sail coming from Mulege with my mother on board.

While Don Justo was spending a few days with us, he sent me on his mule with a message to the well man about two miles from the sea coast. Knowing how I would go to the coast at every chance he warned me not to do it this time. When I found myself only two miles from it I decided to go, thinking Don Justo would never know it. However, to save time I took a short cut through a salt water marsh that looked dry on top; but, when the mule stepped into it its legs sank right down to its knees and I had a hard time getting out of it. The mud was like molasses and it stuck to the mule's legs clear up to its belly.

You may imagine how Don Justo felt when I returned with his mule in that condition. I expected a terrible whipping but he did not go that far.

A few days after that my mother returned and did not again leave us.

While waiting for my father to return we would expend our evenings listening to stories that my mother would tell us and learning simple songs. I always had a good ear for music and from the time

I was four or five years old I could learn tunes and knew a number of songs that my mother would ask me to sing. Many of those old songs were sad and sentimental. A few were folly and comical. I still remember some of them but seldom try to sing them. They bring memories that usually choke my voice.

My trips to Santa Agueda continued regularly. During the pitahaya season [the time when fruit on columnar cacti is ripe] I would take one of my burros to Sta. Agueda with a pair of *argenas* [large leather bags]. I would have a long bamboo pole with a needle point on the end and a chisel-like palette back of this point four inches lower. The pitahaya is a delicious cactus fruit the size of an apple. In Lower California in the southern part several kinds of pitahayas grow in profusion. Some have a deep red heart; others are yellow and others white.

A man came to the mine one day and traded with my mother for a lot of dry cowhides that remained from the time the mine was operating. He gave us fifty pounds of sun dried dates for each hide and the dates came already packed in *surrones* [hide bags]. So we had more dates than we would use in a long time.

At last my father came back by water. He had a position as super-intendent at the *Real del Castillo* mines, not far south of San Diego. He had gone to San Francisco to have some dental work done and from there by steamer to La Paz, Lower California; from La Paz to Mulege; and from Mulege to the beach near our mine in a small sail boat.

It was certainly a great day when he arrived home after being away from us for over a year. He brought me a tin flute and showed me how to play the scale on it.

While stopping at La Paz he met an old friend, Mr. Rabago, who had a flat bottom schooner shipping cattle across the Gulf from Sinaloa. The schooner had a capacity for 50 head and it was a good business to buy the cattle in Sinaloa at a very low price and sell them at La Paz at a good price. Mr. Rabago induced my father to mail his resignation to *El Real del Castillo* mines and bring his family to La Paz, a nice little city with an ideal climate and good schools, and organize a wholesale meat business in partnership with Rabago. My father saw a good field there for this business and with Rabago's capital he decided that it would pay him to go into it.

When he came home to us he told my mother that we would have to be in Mulege to take the next steamer for La Paz. We had a considerable amount of mining tools like wheelbarrows, crow bars, drills, sledges, shovels, picks, etc. Also the house furniture, none of which could be sold readily. The only boat available was an open fishing boat with two men to man it, a single mast and sail. We could only take our trunks with such things as we could pack in them and some bedding. Everything else was left with Doña Reyes at the mine. We loaded our things on pack mules to take them to the coast.

We all piled into this sail open boat and made sail towards Mulege 40 miles away. We had a strong wind behind us. One of the men did nothing but bail water from the bottom of the boat and in about three hours we were landing at Mulege. It was a rough little sea voyage that made my mother deathly sick.

The trip on this steamer was very enjoyable for us boys and my father. La Paz is a very picturesque little city. We went to Mr. Rabago's home and found that he had left with his schooner for Sinaloa after a load of cattle. My father rented a house across the street from the public school. It had no furniture so we had to camp making the beds on the floor.

When my mother went to prepare the first meal for us we discovered that there were no knives nor forks. She had packed a few dishes in the trunks and some pans and pots, but forgot the knives and forks. I cleaned some fish for her with the pieces of glass from a broken bottle. In a couple of days my father had a few things brought to the house, a table, some benches, two or three chairs, some canvas folding cots, and we got along better. His funds were very limited, and the second day in La Paz another friend that he met told him that Rabago was very unreliable and that he seldom kept his word.

My father waited to hear from Rabago but he never came back from Sinaloa while we were in La Paz. He would send an occasional boat load of cattle to one of the butchers but he never would come himself. So my father found himself stranded in a strange town with his family and no funds.

He was too proud to write to the Real del Castillo Mining Co. for the position he had resigned, and I think that he felt he had made a serious mistake by depending on a verbal agreement instead of making Mr. Rabago sign a good contract with him before changing his plans and giving up his position.

My father, like many educated Germans, was a linguist. His friend knew that and suggested that he could give private lessons in English and French to a number of men who he knew would be interested. So my father did that very thing in La Paz for over a year to make a living.

A Mr. Félix Gibert, who owned a number of ships and other valuable properties, wanted to install a pumping station at an orchard he had near the city and lay a pipe line to the port to sell water to the ships. The people of La Paz, like in many other Mexican towns, obtained their water supply from private wells, many of them on the main streets. These were open wells only a few feet to water and anyone could take his own bucket with ten or fifteen feet of rope to draw his water from these public wells. The rich families had windmills, but these were very few.

Most of them used a long beam hung in the middle from a cross bar over two posts near the well. The beam had a bucket hanging by a rope on the end over the well and a rock or some other counter-weight on the other end. To draw the water one would force the rope end with the bucket into the well and when the bucket filled with water the counterbalance on the other end of the pole lever would lift the water out.

Don Félix Gibert heard that my father was an engineer and knew something about machinery. He asked him to install his water plant; also to move some forty or fifty good size orange trees and transplant them in this orchard where they could be irrigated with the power pump. I remember this work very well. The engine was a two cylinder, hot air type, and they used Brazil nuts (*coquitos*) for fuel.

For each orange tree they dug a hole 10 feet in diameter and four or five feet deep. Many of the trees were in bloom and had oranges the same year.

After my father finished this work for Don Félix Gibert he went with a two masted schooner, "*El Salvatierra*," to Ahome, Sinaloa, to purchase a shipload of wheat for Mr. Gibert. In the meantime, he took care of several students who were taking private lessons in English and French.

I was sent with my brother, Dick, to the public school across the street from our home. The teacher was a retired priest, Padre Pedroza, said to be a very fine teacher. We had the usual trouble of all newcomers with the tomboys until we established ourselves. A good many of my own difficulties were while trying to defend my younger brother, Dick, who was always getting himself into quarrels.

My father was a lover of music and wanted me to start learning it as early as possible. There was a private school in La Paz conducted by Father Arce. It was called a college. They had a number of boarding students from several of the other towns in the peninsula besides the day scholars; a music department for sight reading (*solfeo*); band and orchestra instruments; a manual training teacher; an art teacher for drawing; and four or five other teachers for the various school courses.

I was sent to the music class every afternoon after public school hours to take *solfeo*. When I had been going for that a few months my father decided to place me there as a boarder for the better schooling and discipline. My brother, Dick, also went as a day scholar.

I attended this school as a boarder for a year, until my mother received a letter advising her that her father had died without leaving a will and calling her to come at once to see about the distribution of the estate.

While attending Padre Arce's college I again took English. The English teacher was a graduate of Santa Clara College. His name was Salvador Solario. On Sunday afternoon we were taken for walks along the beach and out in the country. At times we were served chocolate at some country home of friends of the school. We were never permitted to go out of the school grounds alone to any place.

The rector was very kind and all the boys loved him, but he was also a very strict disciplinarian.

While waiting for a sailboat to take us back to Guaymas, I was taken out of Padre Arce's school and put in my time walking out into the country to gather wild plums, a very sweet yellow fruit the size of a large olive, yellow in color when ripe and containing a very delicious kernel that the boys would gather after eating the plums and sell to the food stores by the pound as we would peeled almonds. I would also go to the bay to spear sardines which are very plentiful in La Paz Bay. I would make my own spears from old umbrella wires.

In those days, the wire nails that we have now were not used. They had only square nails made of black iron. Around the waterfront where they did some ship work we could find some of these black square nails or spikes. I took one home with me, about six inches long, half inch square at the head and tapering to 1/4" x 3/8" at the end. I managed to grind the end of this spike in the shape of a wood chisel and used it to dig out the hulls of toy boats that I would shape first with my mother's kitchen knives.

One day I was laboring hard on one of these toy boats with my nail chisel as a carpenter coming out of my father's English class passed me, and when he saw what I was doing he invited me to his shop a few blocks away. He shaped the outside of my 4" x 4" redwood block into a perfect racing yacht and then loaned me one of his razor edge wood chisels and a mallet for me to cut out the inside and finish the job. I had been doing this with the little hull placed on my knees when some of the carpenters started playing. I looked around towards them and with my eyes away from my work I missed the block and drove the chisel through my trousers into the flesh above my knee clear to the bone. I was too proud to let the carpenter boys know what I had done and remained seated cutting away until the hull was gouged out. When I stood up my shoe was full of blood. I sneaked out to the bay four blocks away where I rolled up my pants and discovered that I had a real gash in my leg. I washed the blood with sea water and limped home. I was afraid to frighten my mother if I would tell her about it, but she soon discovered something was wrong and I was put to bed.

As soon as I could get out of bed I finished my little yacht. I made a deck for it and rigged it with one mast and two satin sails. I got a strip of lead, nailed it along the keel, made a rudder and it proved to be a perfect sailor. Of course, this was due to the shape of the hull made for it by my carpenter friend.

I had a lot of pleasure playing in the bay with this little yacht.

Adjoining our back yard fence was an orchard with coconut palms and tamarindos, a sweet sour fruit used for making a lemonade-like drink, very refreshing. Also we had in our yard two very large *huamochil* trees. The tree grows as large as an oak and the fruit is a pod about three times as large as a pea pod. The meat is white like that of an apple and very sweet.

A family of Americans came to La Paz about this time. They were farmers or miners. The father, the mother, a daughter about 12, a boy of 14, and another boy of about my age. They found themselves stranded without means and not knowing Spanish. My father helped them to get living quarters in a vacant house near ours. My mother would send me with corn bread and coffee for them and I soon made friends with the boys. They made slingshots and showed me how to use one. They could kill doves and other birds for their mother to cook. One day while the younger boy and I were romping in our back yard I tore his shirt. I will never forget how he cried telling me it was the only shirt he had. I took him in the house and my mother mended his shirt before he went home.

He was my first American friend and I felt very lonesome when they left. The American Consul arranged passage for them in some ship for the U.S.

My two years in La Paz will always be remembered as very happy ones. Across the street from us lived the Palaez family. Their son and daughter played piano and cornet. We could hear them practicing every day. They played parts of *Poet and Peasant Overture.* I played it myself many times years later and always loved it. When I hear it my mind usually goes back to the years of 1878 & 79 at La Paz.

Ships loaded with bananas would come into port and call on the boys to help unload. The pay would be a small bunch of delicious bananas. They would sell at La Paz for one cent apiece.

One time a storm at sea drove several whales into shallow water near the port. The sailors that found them made small fortunes out of them.

The day came for us to sail in a two masted schooner from La Paz to Guaymas. My father remained in La Paz to wind up his school.

Our schooner anchored to take rock ballast at Pichilinge, a small harbor near La Paz where the U.S. has a coaling station. The water at Pichilinge is crystal clear. Our ship was over 20 or 25 feet of water and we could see the bottom full of starfish and other shells. This ship was to load up with salt at Carmen Island located in the Gulf about half way between La Paz and Guaymas. It took two days to make Carmen Island. We anchored about a half mile from shore. A family of Negroes was living there taking care of the mounds of salt. About 8 or 10 little children without any clothes lined the shore when we anchored.

The rock ballast was dumped overboard and the sailors started with two row boats and a barge manned by the island Negroes hauling the salt in sacks to the ship. My brother Dick and I went ashore with the first boat and took a walk over the valley of salt before the sun was up. When the sun started shining over the salt we had a hard time groping our way back to the boats.

The ship loaded, we started for Guaymas. The following day one of the sailors speared two dorado fishes. These are deep water fish about two feet long and about a 4 inch oval around their middle, a very fine fish with hardly any bones. That day we had a banquet on board. My poor mother did not enjoy it, however. She was prostrated with seasickness all the time.

We arrived at Guaymas in due time and stopped at the home of Don Gabriel Corrella, a very dear friend of my father. We had to wait in Guaymas several days until my mother could find a suitable road wagon and driver to take us to Altar.

During those days at Guaymas I would go to the beach to play with my little sail boat. The Guaymas boys had not changed their antagonism against strange boys and it was not long before I had to defend myself and my little boat from two young ruffians who knocked me down before I realized what was up. Fortunately, I was strong enough to keep them off. After that they left me alone.

The wagon which my mother hired for our long trip from Guaymas to Altar was the regulation four spring wagon with two wide seats over a body seven feet long, 4 feet wide, and 10 inches deep, with a standing top covered with white sail duck rolling curtains on the sides and back, a leather dash in front and drawn by two horses. The seats were large enough for six passengers, including the driver.

The first day out of Guaymas we rested the horses at noon and had our lunch at a very fine ranch. I only remember that the woman of the ranch asked Dick and me to take five or six baby dogs to the back of the corrals and kill them as she did not want so many. I remember taking the puppies away to a large mesquite tree and leaving them there to die. I can still feel the awful sensation of that act. I hope the mother dog found them and saved them.

After a few days of travel and camping outdoors (we had bedding with us in the wagon and also food to last us for a few days), we arrived at Hermosillo. There we stopped at the home of another friend and relative, Tía Virginia Romero. They had a very large home with a large patio (court) in the center planted to roses, oranges and other semitropical plants on the order of all the best homes in Mexico. There our baby brother Joe developed a high fever and we had to stay several days hoping that he would get well. Our driver became very restless and threatened to return with his wagon to Guaymas unless we would resume the trip at once.

My mother, with limited funds, was afraid to let him go so we started while the baby was still feverish. On the road to Altar we had two or three heavy summer rain storms and one night we had to stop on the road and spend the night in the wagon. When we finally reached Altar Joe was a very sick baby. He developed a severe case of croup. There was no doctor in Altar. The nearest one at Caborca, 25 miles away, was an American druggist. My mother sent a man on horseback to bring this man to see the baby. When he came, Joe thought he was my father and caressed the man's face with his little hands. He could only smile. There was nothing that could be done and poor little Joe choked to death that night.

This nearly killed my mother. She was about to give birth to my brother Pepe. Pepe was born the night of Dec. 24, 1879, a few days after the first Joe died.

He was my father's pet, and several weeks after he was buried my mother received a letter my father had written to her the day after we left La Paz saying how lonesome he had felt when he left us on the ship and that he dreamed that night that the baby had fallen overboard and drowned. He said that he could not forget the dream and the feeling that he would never see the baby again.

My mother found the estate of her father, Don José María Redondo, in a turmoil. Her stepmother, Doña Dolores Pérez de Redondo, and her son Florencio were in possession of the property. My grandfather Redondo had left the Buzani ranch with a good number of cattle; farm lands in several parts of the state of Sonora; horses in Altar, San Ignacio, Tubutama, Pitiquito, and Oquitoa; an orchard in the suburbs of Altar; and cash deposited with several mercantile houses in Hermosillo and Guaymas. In those days there were no banks in Sonora and it was the custom to deposit cash with the larger merchants and draw "*libranzas*," drafts, against these deposits.

The probating and distribution of my grandfather's estate was a very long and complicated procedure. It remained in the courts for several years, and in the end the bulk of it was absorbed by lawyers' fees and expenses. Of course, Doña Lola, my grandfather's widow, and her son Florencio, a half wit, retained the greatest portion of what was left. My mother was given the orchard near Altar and about 100 acres of farm land adjoining. This property had a water right in the gravity ditch from the Altar River and was considered a very good farm.

While this farm was made ready to turn over to my mother, we lived in town at Antonio Redondo's home, a cousin of my mother who was married to my half-sister, Maggie. I was sent to the public school conducted then by Don Jesús Anguez, a very tall, dark man of dignified appearance and considered a fine scholar. The school was the same one I had known in 1875 when Don Félix Rodríguez was the teacher.

My first day in school Don Jesús Anguez gave me a short examination and when I read a few paragraphs from a history of the U.S.-Mexican war, he stopped me and called the class to order. I was scared not knowing what was coming. He told the boys to listen to my reading and made me stand in front and read to the class for a few minutes. I realized then that he approved of my reading and wanted his boys to notice it. He assigned me to my grade and for several months for my Spanish reading class he would ask me to read for him from the same history of the war between the U.S. and Mexico. Some days some particular chapter would interest him and he would ask me to read on several more pages.

For penmanship and writing his method was to make us copy from some well-written book. I always felt that this was a good practical way to acquire good style in composition and learn to spell and punctuate correct Spanish.

From La Paz I had brought a game that the boys played similar to what we know as Keno. There it was called "*Lotería*," an oblong sheet of cardboard with as many squares with different figures as the number of cards in a Mexican deck. Similar figures would be pasted on the face of the cards. Two squares on the sheet would have one and two circles. The square with the single circle was called "*casa chica*," and the one with the two circles, "*Casa Grande*." The dealer or owner of the *Lotería* would shuffle the cards, place the deck face down on the board or table, and invite the players to place their marbles as in a roulette table, selecting whatever figure they would like. When all the marbles were placed, the deck of cards would be cut and turned up, as when playing "*albures*," Faro. The figures covered by marbles would win an equal number from the bank, but when "*casa chica*" or "*Casa Grande*" would come, all the remaining marbles on the card would be lost to the bank. The novelty of this game took the boys by storm and in a few days I had about a three-gallon bucket of marbles of all descriptions.

We had a large back yard and it occurred to me that this was a good place to hold a circus, "*maromas*." This back yard was enclosed by high adobe walls on the four sides with a gate to the back street. My mother and my father had always encouraged us in gymnastics and acrobatics. My mother made clown suits for Dick and me, short trunks and jackets, red and green. We set up a horizontal bar and planted four long posts with poles tied across the tops from which we hung trapezes and rings. We invited four or five other boys who could do tricks on the bar and turn cartwheels, balance on the trapeze, etc. until we had what we imagined a good program of acrobatic stunts. I borrowed a burro and used one of my mother's pillows and a blanket to improvise a pad on the burro's back for equestrian stunts and would have one of the boys lead the burro around the corral while one of us would stand up on the burro's back and mimic a circus rider.

We had everything ready for the first performance on a Saturday night. The admission was one cigarette. For lighting the circus we did what we had seen the Mexican circus do: set up a post in the ground about four feet high, fasten an adobe as best we could across the top of the post, and with dry cactus centers that we could bring in from the neighboring hills would build a fire on the adobe. The dry cactus wood would burn like paper and make a good size torch. Four of those in charge of a boy that would feed the fires continuously going from one to the other would give us a splendid illumination for the performance.

My sister Maggie had a house boy who was not a boy but an undersized man with a full red beard and very serious and silent. His name was Jesusito. He had helped us to borrow ropes and poles to set up our apparatus and was very much interested in circus activities. He told me that he had a violin, that he could play it, and would like to play for our performance if I could get a nickel for him to buy rosin for his bow. I knew that this poor fellow was a simpleton, but harmless and always willing to help, a 40-year-old dwarf with a very serious face and demeanor, and the mentality of a child. My mother gave me a bit for him. He fixed his fiddle and we were all set.

The torches on the adobes were lighted and the boys started coming in with their cigarettes for admission. The clown came out from the side door followed by the troop of acrobats, four or five boys dressed up in different outfits, some with their mothers' or sisters' stockings to appear as if wearing tights. The clown delivered his announcement in verse and I climbed to a trapeze for the first stunt. I was hanging on my knees when Jesusito started to play a tune on his fiddle known as *La Liebre* (The Jackrabbit). I had forgotten all about him, and his tune, played all out of tune, sounded so terribly funny to me that I had to slide down to the ground with a hysterical fit of laughter that just about ended the feast.

Anyway, we had a good time. But we never repeated the performance. We kept the apparatus and enjoyed playing on it until we moved to the farm.

At this farm we had a very small house, two rooms, a kitchen, and a porch, but in front of the house we had six tremendously large ash trees. The tops of these trees were as one and in the shade of these beautiful trees we lived most of the time. The orchard had figs, pears, pomegranates, quinces, dates, and about two acres in grapes. All these fruits did well, particularly the figs and grapes.

While my father's profession was mining, he had studied horticulture and knew a good deal about trees, flowers, vegetables, and general farming. We soon had a vegetable patch with a large variety. I used to get my fill of radish and carrots. One of the date palms near the house would have large bunches of delicious dates in season and Dick and I would fight to climb up to the bunches and pick the ripe ones.

There was a pond in the back of the house deep enough for diving. I could turn a back somersault from the bank into the water. We would fill this pond with water from the ditch and it was one of our greatest pleasures. Here I learned to plow, to irrigate, hoe and spade the soil. I would walk to school about a mile and after school hours I would help with the farm work. We had a milk cow and it was my duty to cut hay for it, water it, milk it, and take care of it. I made a lot of small adobes about the size of our brick and built a play room with them. I also built a small oven where I used to bake pumpkins. I would cut a hole into the pumpkin, take out all the seeds, put in a broken *panocha* (brown sugar cake), and when the pumpkin was taken out of the oven and cut in two halves we would fill the halves with milk and eat it all with a spoon.

My father let me have a muzzle loading double barrel shot gun, powder, shot, and caps. I learned to handle it and would go out hunting. I never forgot my first cottontail and how proudly I brought it home to my mother.

One morning I found a horse lying on the ground by a bunch of wheat straw left from the harvest. It was so poor and weak that he could not get up. I went home and brought a bucket of water and some corn which I gave him while he was down. He took it all and I went after more for him.

I came back in the evening and found the horse up on his feet. I led him home and fed him a few days. When he appeared to have gained strength I saddled him and found that he was a good saddle horse and very gentle. He had a fresh brand, "E.S.", meaning "Estado de Sonora." A troop of cavalry passing by had left him when he was too weak to use. The horse got strong to work both in the saddle and also pulling a pony plow, but he was always bony. We had used him for some time when a man named José María Noriega from Pitiquito came to see us. I was called in to meet him. He thanked me for having saved his favorite horse. He said he had heard all about it.

I thought here is where I lose my horse, but to my surprise he told me to keep it as a present from him. This horse was a great pleasure and comfort to me.

We had a two wheel light cart for general work on the farm. One morning I was driving in this cart to town to get some supplies when I heard a volley of rifle fire in the court of Tía María Antonia's home where a troop of soldiers were making their barracks. I stopped the cart against the wall and stood on the edge of the side boards to peep into the courtyard. Just as I was looking at three men dead on the ground, a soldier fired three shots into their heads. This is called *"el tiro de gracia"* [coup de grace] when executions are made in Mexico by shooting. This frightened me terribly and I started for the farm, but just as I was turning into the road a soldier stopped me and ordered me off the cart and he climbed into it and drove away. I ran home as fast as my legs would carry me, told my father about the episode, and he said there was nothing to worry about. The soldiers would return the cart and horse to us when they were through with it. Sure enough, they brought it back several hours later with the bottom of the body covered with blood. They had used it to take the bodies of the three men to the graveyard.

We never used that cart again.

I was riding my horse bareback one afternoon over a country trail when he stumbled over a mesquite root. I went over its head and when I got up the horse was standing and shaking with pain. I led him home and it took the rest of the afternoon to walk only about two miles. The horse had sprained his front left foot and could hardly walk. As soon as we got home he lay down groaning with pain. My father applied a liniment for several days and as soon as he could walk we turned him loose into the wheat field. He got well and fat eating green wheat hay for several weeks.

For San Juan's Day I caught him and staked him in a field of ripe barley so I could saddle him the next morning. When I went after him I found him dead. He had evidently eaten too much barley grain with the barbs. The horse died on the night of June 22d.

On June 24 was to be San Juan's Day when everybody that can get a horse or mule or burro was supposed to ride. I caught a young burro and saddled him. It behaved quite well after a few hours so I thought I was fixed up for my San Juan celebration the next day. I tied the burro under a tree and gave him a good ration of hay for the night. Next morning when I saddled him he jumped and kicked and twisted into knots until he fell on his back. My father told me to turn him loose, fearing that his good saddle would not stand much more. So I did not have my ride after all.

About this time Professor Salcedo had been engaged by several of the Altar families to conduct a private school for their children. Of course my father placed me with Professor Salcedo. They were old time friends. Here we had boys and girls, many of them young ladies, and boys—16 to 20 years old. The classes were reading, penmanship, arithmetic, algebra and geometry for the higher students, geography, history, Spanish grammar, English, music, sight reading and drawing.

While attending this school a boy about my age, Panchito Heras, and I were going to fight a duel. Seconds were named and we all walked to the river where we were to fight. Panchito was a nice fellow and anything but a fighting boy. I have never had a belligerent disposition myself, so the seconds had no difficulty in reconciling us. We shook hands and walked back to school better friends than before.

A German boy named Waldemar Mueller was placed in this school to learn Spanish. He could only talk English and German. Prof. Salcedo would ask me to go with Waldemar by his home every day after school. His parents, Dr. & Mrs. Mueller, and a baby sister, Meta, lived near the flour mill located out of town and only about 1/2 mile from our orchard home. These walks with Waldemar gave me a chance to practice my English.

Prof. Salcedo never liked Altar and his school was discontinued after the first year. Many of us went back to the public school with Don Jesús Anguez. A musician from Durango, Don Lazaro Valencia, was then teaching *solfeo*, music sight reading, and singing. The boys in his class were paying 5 dollars (pesos) per month for one hour lesson in class every day excepting Saturdays and Sundays from 5 to 6 P.M. He used the *solfeo* method of Gómez, a famous Spanish teacher of music. This was an expensive book that very few of the boys could afford to purchase. Don Lazaro discovered that.

I knew several lessons of the first part of the Gómez method and suggested that I would help him to write the music lesson for the class for my own tuition. I would write on Saturdays, copying from his book, and help the boys at class. I think this gave me a foundation that otherwise would have been more difficult to obtain. After I had learned to sight read in all the seven clefs, Don Lazaro started me learning to play the flute. A lawyer named Ignacio Bustillas had a five-key rosewood German flute of the old Meyer system. He was good enough to lend it to me and this was the instrument which I used to learn the fingering and tone producing. The wood was cracked in several places and I had to fill the cracks with beeswax. I also had to make new pads out of old kid gloves for the keys. My hands were hard and calloused from the work I had to do on the farm and Don Lazaro would wonder at times if I would ever be able to do much with my stiff fingers.

During school vacation I worked at the farm. I would take the flute with me and practice while irrigating and at every other chance I had. When I returned to school Don Lazaro was surprised with the advance I had made in fingering and tone.

He organized a quintet consisting of double bass, guitar, and a saxhorn for harmony and flute and cornet for melody. He played the cornet himself and I will never forget his beautiful mellow tone. I played the flute in this quintet. It was not long before we were in demand for serenades and other functions. The rates were one dollar per hour for each member. I thought this was a fortune for me.

By this time my father had been called by Governor Don Carlos Ortiz to Hermosillo where he offered the office of *Perito de Minas,* mining advisor, for the District of Magdalena. The duties of that office were to issue titles on mines, survey the claims, direct the works, and inspect the mines twice a year to see that operations were conducted according to law and the safety of the miners. The fees for this work averaged better than $500. per month.

My father accepted this appointment and decided to take us to

Magdalena as soon as we could rent or sell the orchard & farm. In the meantime, I was helping to take care of the crops we had growing. We had a Yaqui laborer who did most of the harder work excepting when we had to irrigate day and night. He would take the night shift and I would handle the water in the daytime. Sometimes, however, he would play sick and I had to work nights and let him work in the daytime, particularly when the nights were cold enough to freeze the water as it spread over the lands.

We could not afford to hire more than one hand and I had to supply the extra help. Here is where I learned to plow, hoe the weeds, irrigate, cut hay with a sickle, milk a cow, and do any other chore required. I was then 12 to 13 years old but large and strong for my age.

My mother had been offered a price for the crop by a man named Sr. Chavarín, a rather stout and flashy gentleman, also to rent the farm. His offer was accepted and he came over with two farm hands ready to take over the watering which I had been handling for three days and two nights because our Yaqui was either sick or playing so. Of course, I must have been dead tired, getting sleep only in snatches between lands and hoping that Mr. Chavarín would close his deal and relieve me when to my dismay I noticed that he and his two laborers were leaving. He had changed his proposition and my mother had refused to accept the change, but she saw the look of distress in my face. She called Mr. Chavarín back and turned the place over to him and his men. This she told me afterwards.

We moved into town to await for my father to send for us. I left school then and that was the last time I ever attended any school. I was not quite 13.

Don Lazaro, my music teacher, continued to call me for playing at $1 per hour. I would give the money to my mother and she consented reluctantly, knowing that we would soon leave Altar.

One night while we were serenading for account of one of the prominent men of the town, a fight was started by two of the men in the party. Shots were fired and the police arrested these men. That was the end of my playing with Don Lazaro's quintet for money. My mother would not let me go anymore.

Before leaving school in Altar, I had two sad experiences. One time fighting with another boy by throwing rocks at each other, one of mine hit a poor hunchback boy in the head and nearly killed him. I ran to him and picked him up with a cut in his scalp over an inch long. I never will forget the feeling of remorse that I suffered for days until the boy was well enough to return to school. His name was José María López. He was older than I and a very good student, always at the head of the class in arithmetic. Many years later in one of my trips to Cananea I met him there doing well. He remembered the incident of the rock and showed me the scar.

Another time, playing at wrestling with a boy named Francisco Sotelo, a friend of mine (he and I used to whistle duets for hours in the evenings), he lost his head and slashed my left wrist with a shoemaker's knife that he carried in his pocket. When we met again in school, we shook hands and made friends again. I still have the scar to remember him by.

Another time I took a boy named Santiago Redondo, a son of an uncle of my mother, for a hunting trip. I had a double barrel muzzle loading shot gun. We found a good place to shoot doves between a water hole and a ditch about 500 feet apart. I would shoot at the doves coming to water at the ditch and then walk to the water hole to shoot them when they would come there. Santiago would pick them up for me. In passing by him one of my barrels went off and set his overalls on fire near his foot. I took his shoe off and found that a number of the shot had entered his heel. I had to carry him home. He got well but always limped after that. Some muscle must have been injured.

About this time my father had been appointed *Perito de Minas* (Director and Inspector of Mines) for the District of Magdalena. On his way home from Hermosillo during a stormy night the stage was upset while fording a flooded part of the road near Santa Ana. My father, with the other passengers, suffered from exposure in the cold water and developed a serious case of fever and other complications that nearly took his life.

Magdalena had no hospital or any other facilities so my father sent his driver to Altar to bring me over to help. There was not a doctor in Magdalena. A drug store owned by an old American druggist, Don Alejandro Clark, furnished the only medical aid possible. My father's case required changing hot flaxseed poultices for several days and nights and this was my work. When he recovered enough to leave his bed, he rented a house from Don Pancho Gallego. While the place was made ready, he sent me to Altar after my mother and the children, Dick, Emilia, and Pepe. I drove my father's mountain road wagon, the type made on four springs, two seats for six passengers and a good storm top with side curtains. The two horse team made the 60 miles from Magdalena to Altar in two short days. As my mother was ready, we loaded as much of our things as could be packed in the road wagon, trunks and bedding on the trunk rack in the back, and started for Magdalena. We made El Ocuca before night.

El Ocuca was the original settlement of the first Redondo that came to Mexico from Spain, my mother's great grandfather.[5] There we camped for the night.

One of my grand uncles, Don Esteban Redondo, who still held his interest in the ranch, was staying there at the time after locating a large herd of cattle that he had driven there from Yuma, Arizona to save them from an Arizona drought of the previous years. Don Esteban Redondo and family were then residents of Yuma. His oldest daughter, Doña Delfina, had married Dr. George Martin, the father of Andy & Geo. Martin of Tucson. Another daughter of Tío Esteban Redondo, still living in Tucson, is the widow of Andrés Rebeil and mother of Julia, Paul, and Steve Rebeil.

Tío Esteban came over to our camp the next morning and had breakfast with us. My mother had provided the *bastimento* (lunch) for the trip, such things as were used at that time: *carne seca con chile* [jerked beef with chile], *tortillas de leche* [tortillas made with milk], cheese, and coffee.

We left El Ocuca after breakfast and arrived at Magdalena in the evening before dark.

An American friend of my father who heard that I played the flute sent me a very nice instrument, with his compliments, from Tucson. He also sent my father a beautifully engraved and nickle plated Winchester carbine. My father had helped him in connection with some mining work and he showed his appreciation by sending these fine presents.

It was not long before the young people of Magdalena discovered that I could play the flute. Santiago Campbell, a boy whose father was an old friend of my father, played the guitar. We practiced a repertoire of the pieces that I knew by heart, songs, danzas, serenades, waltzes, mazurkas, schottisches, polkas, etc., and in a few weeks we were able to furnish flute and guitar music for our friends' parties and serenades. Of course we were in demand and these few months of my stay in Magdalena were certainly very happy ones.

My father bought a large lot with an old house that was rebuilt for us and we were soon settled in a home of our own. We had a nice patio and garden and a large *"trascorral"*—back yard and stable. My father had a good saddle horse and his two horses for the road wagon.

While I was 14 years old and my schooling had been very limited, there was no chance in Magdalena as the public school was a very poor one and only for small children of the first grades. So my time was occupied by helping my father. I would go with him on his trips of inspection to the mines. Many beautiful spots were visited on these trips.

I will never forget a few days we stayed at the Aguaje Canyon near a mine which my father was inspecting. I had nothing to do but shoot with my father's engraved Winchester and tramp over the canyon, resting as I desired under the *aliso's* [alder's] shade by the crystal like water flowing over the rocks.

While in town I used to ride my father's saddle horse to San Ignacio and down the Magdalena River to San Lorenzo and Santa Ana. I had a favorite *"ondable,"* water hole, north of the town where I could swim.

This idyllic life could not last forever. My father had planned to send me to Philadelphia to learn the ship building trade. He had a friend connected with one of the large shipyards who had offered to look after me. My mother had protested when my father had wanted to send me to Mexico City to a preparatory school for the military college where President Juárez had granted him a *"beca"* (scholarship) for one of his boys. She did not want any more soldiers in the family. I was disappointed but now I know how sound her judgement was.

Both finally compromised on sending me to Tucson where Mr. [Winnall] Dalton and his brother-in-law, Adolfo Vásquez, were operating a carriage shop. The carriage and wagon industry was a major one in those days and my parents decided that I could do well in that line. Mrs. Dalton was my mother's cousin, and I was to live at their home while serving my apprenticeship.

While waiting to be taken to the U.S., I occupied my time hunting rabbits, doves, and quail in the foothills near Magdalena. I also made some stools and benches for my mother at the carpenter shop of our neighbors Alberto and Alejandro Barreda. Mrs. Barreda's maiden name was Elías of the old Elías family, founders of the town of Arizpe from which we know at the present day, Pancho Elías, ex-governor of Sonora, and one of Ex-President Calles' right hand men. One of our great grandmothers was an Elías and my mother always recognized these blood relations and we were taught to know them as *parientes* (relatives) in the well established Spanish custom. A *pariente* even in the fourth or fifth degree is a blood relative and must be recognized as such. Therefore about half of the people of Sonora are descendants from the Redondos, Vásquez, Urreas, and the Elíases. We have an army of blood relatives (*parientes*).

One day two German friends of my father returning from Europe arrived at Magdalena by the Tucson stage. The stage from Magdalena to Hermosillo was not leaving until two or three days later, and my father sent these friends in his own road wagon to the Santa Fe Rail Road camp which was located then near La Noria south of Santa Ana. This Railroad was being built from Guaymas to Benson [ca. 1881]. My father's driver, Juan de Dios, drove the team, and I was invited to go along. We arrived at the camp after dark. I was surprised to find the rails made as they were. I had imagined railroad rails to be channeled. When I saw that they were not steel channels, I thought surely that the locomotive and car wheels had to be channeled to stay on the road. When the work train came in about midnight, the locomotive appeared to me as a tremendous monster (as a matter of fact, it was a very small wood burning engine, a type common at that time).

When I got over my surprise I walked close enough to notice the wheels had no channels or rims. It was a great puzzle for me. The train kept moving until it backed away toward Guaymas, and in the dark I had no chance to notice the inside wheel flanges. We went right back to Magdalena and my father had to explain to me what it was that kept the train wheels on the track. However it was not altogether clear to me until I came to Tucson and saw the S. P. [Southern Pacific Railroad] Locomotives in action.

In Magdalena I worked in the wagon and carpenter shop of Don Manuel Martínez, whose shop was located in part of the large home of the Monroys. Rafael Monroy married a cousin of my mother, Chonita Redondo, and as they were also related to the Gallego family their home was always a gathering place for a lot of young people. Don Pancho Gallego had six beautiful daughters. The most beautiful, Toña, was three or four years older than myself. I used to dream myself in love with her. She was very white with beautiful brown eyes and a wealth of light brown hair. Two years later she came with her father to Tucson and I was disappointed when I saw her all dressed up and wearing a hat that did not become her a bit. Toña Gallego ceased to be my ideal of a beautiful girl.

Her younger sisters were good looking also, and so were Carolina Monroy, Lupita Aguirre, and Virginia Campbell. I had opportunities to see all of these girls later when they had grown up, but they never looked the same as when I used to see them from Don Manuel's shop.

Don Manuel had a contract to build a concentrating drum out of 6-inch thick mesquite planks. He placed me to rip mesquite logs about 10 feet long by 12 inches thick with a hand saw. This job lasted several weeks and was excellent exercise for my right arm.

One day Don Manuel stayed away from the shop most of the day. He came in late in the afternoon well illuminated with mescal and proceeded to cuss the woodworker that he had left in the shop, and threw the tools around and stormed around everything and everybody. When I went home that evening I told my parents about it and asked them not to let me go to that shop again. My father told me how I should learn to tolerate those episodes common to some of the best mechanics and told me to go back to work. I started out but decided to think it over for a while and I sat down on a large stone which had been placed around the corner of the house where it was shaded from the sun. I had only sat there for a few minutes when my father spoke to me. He had evidently observed my dejection and told me to come back to the house and forget about going back to Don Manuel's shop. A few weeks after that my father started with me for Tucson.

Our driver was Juan de Dios, the same man that my father had for all of his mining trips. The first stop was made at Las Casitas. The Santa Fe R.R. Co. was building the road from Guaymas to Benson. They had a camp of men cutting railroad ties along the road from Imuris to Nogales. As a matter of fact, there was not any Nogales then in April of 1882.

The next day we passed Calabasas. As we crossed into the United

States of America, my father told me, "Now you are in the United States of America, without any question the greatest nation in the world. You will enjoy great liberty and protection under the American Government and you must always feel and show deep appreciation for that. When you become a man (I was fourteen years old at the time), you may want to establish yourself in the United States and see that your life and conduct is such as will entitle you to the privilege of American citizenship." I was impressed by my father's words. My father had served for 22 years as an officer in the Mexican army and I have an idea now, that, while he never expressed it, he must have realized that he might have offered his services to the United States at that time.

Frederick Augustus Ronstadt, the father of
Fred Ronstadt, ca. 1868.

Margarita Redondo
Ronstadt, the mother of
Fred Ronstadt, ca. 1879.
(Courtesy W. E. Ronstadt.)

Left to right: Siblings Richard
and Fred Ronstadt, ca. 1879.

Families of Winnall Dalton and Adolfo Vásquez, ca. 1888. *Left to Right:* Josefa Vásquez, Natalie Dalton, Concepción Suastegui ("Tía Chona"), Hortense Dalton, Winnall Dalton, Henry Dalton, Maria Jesús Vásquez Dalton, Lupe Dalton, Rosa Herras, Amelia Herras Vásquez, and Adolfo Vásquez. The two small children in the right front: Laura and Raul Vásquez. (Courtesy Richard Dalton.)

Fred Ronstadt, ca. 1890

Fred Ronstadt, ca. 1882

Left to right: Rufino Vélez and Fred Ronstadt, ca. 1889

Club Filarmónico Tucsonense, Fred Ronstadt's band, ca. 1896

Wedding portrait of Fred Ronstadt and Sara Levin, his first wife, ca. 1892. (Courtesy Alicia Ronstadt Retes.)

Children of Fred and Sara Levin Ronstadt. *Above left to right:* Laura, Alicia, and Luisa. *Front:* Fred A. (Courtesy Arizona Historical Society.)

Wedding portrait of
Winnall A. Dalton and
Maria Jesús Vásquez
Dalton, October 4, 1878.
They were the parents of
Lupe Dalton, Fred
Ronstadt's second wife.

Lupe Dalton,
bookkeeper at F.
Ronstadt Company,
1903. She and Fred
Ronstadt married
on February 14,
1904.

Fred Ronstadt family, 1924. *Back left to right:* Gilbert, William, and Alfred. *Front left to right:* Fred, Edward, and Lupe.

Luisa Ronstadt Kassler ("Luisa Espinel"), the oldest daughter of Fred and Sara Levin Ronstadt, ca. 1936. She was an internationally reknowned singer and performer.

José María ("Pepe") Ronstadt, brother and business associate of Fred Ronstadt, ca. 1914. He served as postmaster of Tucson during Woodrow Wilson's presidency.

Richard Redondo Ronstadt, Tucson businessman and
brother of Fred Ronstadt, ca. 1903.

Rufino Vélez,
bookkeeper for F.
Ronstadt Company,
ca. 1898. Rufino is
seated at Fred
Ronstadt's desk.

Ronstadt-Zepeda wagon and implement store, ca. 1898

F. Ronstadt Company, 1917. At the time the second story
at the front of the building was Tucson's post office.
José María Ronstadt was postmaster.

Salesroom of
the F. Ronstadt
Company,
1901. The
room behind
the window to
the right was
the general
office.

Yuma stage-
coach made by
the F. Ronstadt
Company.

Horse-drawn streetcar manufactured
in the Ronstadt shops

2
Tucson, Arizona

At that time the International Boundary between Mexico and the U.S. had not been definitely established.[1] The settlers of Calabasas expected the line to run close to them and had made plans for the future border city to be located there. Mr. Wise, father of Joe Wise who is now a prominent citizen of Nogales, had built several houses and a very nice brick hotel in anticipation of the expected boom for his townsite. It was said that Mr. Wise had elaborate calendars advertising his Calabasas city lots with pictures of steamboats running in the Santa Cruz River along the future docks of Calabasas.

It was a great disappointment when the line was found to be five miles to the south and the City of Nogales was founded with its Custom houses and other Port establishments, leaving Calabasas, its beautiful little hotel, its brick houses and all the dreams of Mr. Wise five miles to the north.

Before coming through Calabasas, we passed by Pete Kitchen's ranch. My father had known Pete Kitchen and told me some of the episodes of his life. The country around his ranch was infested with the Apache Indians and Pete Kitchen had many fights with them. At one time he shot an Apache from the front door of his ranch home.

Pete Kitchen was a famous pioneer and many tales about him may be found in the archives of the Arizona Pioneers' Historical Society.[2]

Our next stop was at Tubac, the place where my father had nursed General Pesqueira, the Governor of Sonora, and many others of the General's staff 20 [*sic*] years before [in 1865–1866] when the Maximilian invasion had forced the capital of Sonora to be transferred to Tubac as close to the U.S. as possible, and they all went down with malaria (chills and fever).[3]

Here we visited Sabino Otero who was then living at Tubac. My father also called on his old friend Glassman. Mr. Glassman was an uncle of Colombus Glassman, well known cattleman who lived in Tucson until 1934.

The next morning we started on the last day of our trip. We stopped to get water at Junction, called so because the road to Arivaca joined the Tucson road at this point. At Junction I noticed the Chinese cook of the stage post (change station for the Aguirre stage line) dressed like a cowboy with a large 45 Colt revolver hanging from his belt. We passed the old Canoa Ranch, at that time owned by [Fred] Maish and [Thomas] Driscoll, then Sahuarita, another stage station. Here was Mr. J. K. Brown and his family, another well known [figure] of the early pioneers. One of Mr. Brown's sons, Roy, is still living in the new Sahuarita. One daughter married Hon. Mulford Winsor, another one is Mrs. Miles Carpenter and a third one is living in the old city home on S. Fifth Ave.

We reached the south edge of Tucson about 4 P.M. and drove north along Meyer St. From the time I had seen the new houses at Calabasas, I was struck with the symmetry of the lines. The adobe walls appeared to me to have perfect lines on the corners, and the doorways, also the roofs, were so perfect as compared with the houses that my eyes were used to seeing in Sonora.

Coming to McCormick Street I saw a military looking man riding a beautiful black horse. He was the Tucson City Marshall. His name was Buttner,[4] a tall, lanky man who looked like General von Moltke's pictures. He was known to be a very brave man and a fine officer. He rode his horse ahead of us into Conn's livery stable on Meyer Street. The Carriage and Wagon shop of [Winnall] Dalton and [Adolfo] Vásquez was located in the same block only a few doors north of Conn's livery stable. The old stable and corral is still in the same condition as I write these lines as it was when I came on the 23rd of April 1882.

The wagon and carriage trade at that time and for many years after was a major industry in the U.S. The shop that Dalton and Vásquez had was a plain frame building, but what it lacked in buildings and equipment was made up by skill in the art. Mr. Dalton, himself a man of culture with an excellent background, was an artisan of rare skill. Mr. Vásquez was also a splendid mechanic and they had with them a very fine painter and finisher. His name was Saint Onge. The carriages made in their shop were works of art, made principally from second growth hickory, yellow poplar, Norway iron hand-forgings, and trimmed and painted like the finest furniture.

In the shop of Don Manuel Martínez in Magdalena, the iron forged by hand was rough, and even after straightened by much filing, was still crude and without symmetry or grace. It was a revelation to me to see the beautiful shaped hand forgings perfectly fitted to the wood parts, the graceful lines of the wood work, and most of all, the mirrorlike finish of the carriages. I made up my mind that I was going to learn that trade!

After leaving our wagon and horses at Conn's Stable, we came to [the] Dalton and Vásquez shop. They were both young men in their early thirties. Mr. Dalton wore a full beard, light brown, and Mr. Vásquez only a heavy mustache. Both were handsome specimens of manhood. I thought it strange that they should be wearing working clothes, particularly Mr. Dalton, as he had a very distinguished personality and I knew from hearing it at home that he had come from a very high class family in California and that he was well educated, spoke several languages and was a real gentleman by breeding and education. His Spanish was pure without a trace of accent. I thought this was remarkable knowing that his father was English. I did not know until later that his mother was Spanish from the original Zamoranos that settled California. We were taken to their home . . . . There I met Mrs. Dalton who 22 years later was to be my mother-in-law. Mrs. Dalton was my mother's cousin. That was one of the reasons for my coming to their home. My parents knew their beautiful character and that I would have a real home with them. Mrs. Dalton's mother, Tía Chona [Concepción Suastegui], was then about 45, very vigorous and in complete charge and control of the home. I had seen Tía Chona at Magdalena a few months before when she had gone there to visit her brother, Don Jesús Suastegui. Tía Chona was very methodical. Her house was well managed and she exacted punctuality from everyone but, with all that, she was kind and very charming. I soon learned to love her. However my ideal of a young mother and wife was Mrs. Dalton. At that time she was only 27 years old, a rare beauty, and lovely in every way. Her only baby then was Hortense, about three years old. Lupe, my own wife, came that same year of 1882 in August. It was my privilege to have been sent at midnight to call the midwife that took care of Mrs. Dalton. I was then 14 years old. I never imagined that some day Lupe would be the mother of my four boys.

Tía Chona had a nice garden in the back lot and part of my work was to draw water every evening from a sixty foot well to irrigate the garden. In the morning before breakfast I had to fill the barrels and ollas for the day's supply and carry water to the front of the house to water the trees. I also had to chop fire wood and keep the yard raked. This work together with 10 hours of shop work kept me from mischief. In the shops of that time, we also had to draw water from our wells, as Tucson did not have water works until 1884. For drinking water we would get a few buckets from Joe Phy's water wagon at 5 cents per bucket, and for a hot bath we would go to Sander's Bath House located about the present site of the Carrillo School house. At home I washed from a pail out in the yard through summer and winter. Sometimes we had to break the ice on top of the water tub to get water for washing.

My first year in Tucson, Tía Chona saw to it that I made my First Communion and was confirmed. I was confirmed by Bishop [Jean Baptiste] Salpointe at the old St. Agustín Cathedral on Church Plaza. Part of the old building and the main cut stone entrance still stand. It is now used for a garage. This is a historical landmark that should be preserved.[5]

The prayers that my mother taught me I have always remembered. Morning and night I have always said besides the Lord's Prayer and my Hail Marys,

Gracias alabanzas te doy gran Señor y alabo tu gran poder pues con el alma en el cuerpo me has dejado amanecer. Yo te pido creador mío por tu caridad y amor, me dejas anochecer en gracia y servicio tuyo por siempre jamas, Amen. Angel de mi guarda, amable compañia. No me desampares de noche ni de día. Con Dios me acuesto, con Dios me levanto. Dios con migo, yo con El, Dio delante y yo tras de El.[6]

Then to end I have always said one more short prayer that my father taught me: "*Virgen Purísima cubreme con tu manto celestial* [Most pure Virgin, cover me with your heavenly mantle]," and in the morning, "*Virgen Purísima no me dejes caer en tentacion* [Most pure Virgin, do not let me fall into temptation]."

My father told me about a great sinner who had sold his soul to the devil with the condition that he could take him only while asleep at night. This sinner would never fail to say, "*Virgen Purísima cubreme con tu manto celestial,*" before getting into bed every night and, of course, the devil would always find him covered with the Virgin's mantle and never could take him. My father also told me about a very old woman living in Altar who seemed very tired of this life and would pray fervently every night to the Lord that she be taken to Him. The town joker stopped by this old lady's window one night while she was saying her usual prayer. At the end, he spoke in a sepulchral voice to her from the dark and said, "*Soy un ángel del Señor que vengo por tí* [I am an angel of the Lord who comes for you]." The old lady heard this seeming voice from the other world, and after thinking for a few seconds she answered. "*Oye, ángel del Señor, dile a tu Señor Dios que no estoy aquí, que me fui para Oquitoa* [Listen, angel of the Lord, tell your Lord God that I am not here, that I went to Oquitoa]."

The S.P. [Southern Pacific] Railroad had reached Tucson only about a year before [in March 1880], and many of the large twenty mule freight wagons were still handling freight principally from and to the mining towns. The wagon business was then a major industry and Tucson had three very good wagon shops. Charlie Etchells had the largest. Dalton and Vásquez had theirs on Meyer St. south of Ochoa. A Canadian Frenchman named Gravel had a shop on the corner of Ochoa and Convent. Gravel was considered by far the finest carriage maker here. There was another shop on the corner of Pennington and Meyer. John Mott and James Quinlan, both very good men, owned it. Jimmy Moss who died recently was the horseshoer. Jimmy was married to Mary Lee, daughter of the Jimmy Lee who built the first flour mill and dam at Silver Lake, south of Tucson.

When I came to Tucson the exciting days of the pioneers were about over, and I never experienced anything very exciting. The public lights, gas, were lighted by a man on horseback every evening and put out in the morning. This man, Jack Spencer, is still living in Tucson. The first electric lights were placed on top of high poles about 50 feet high. We had one on the corner of Congress and Sixth Avenue, another on Meyer and Council St. and the third one some place on Stone Avenue and Ochoa. Frank Russell had to climb these poles to change the carbons. They hoped to light the entire city by these three lights but they soon saw that it was a mistake.

After Chief Buttner died, the office was given to Billy Roach. One time a man named George Bundy while drunk had tried to kill a woman across the street from our shop. The woman escaped and ran through our shop to hide in the back paint room. Roach had been called and while trying to arrest Bundy he cracked him over the head with his .44 pistol and knocked him out. While waiting for a carryall to take Bundy to jail, Bundy revived and jumped up and made for Roach. Roach jumped back and leveling the gun at Bundy ordered him to stop but Bundy kept walking towards Roach planning, no doubt, to get close enough to snatch his gun, and Roach's threats to shoot him did not seem to scare him a bit. Roach did not want to kill him and was afraid to let him get too close. I was looking on from the shop door when Roach shouted to me to come and grab Bundy.

As I grew up in Tucson, I was undecided about my ultimate location. My mother had considerable property in Sonora. Some town houses, a very fine farm near Magdalena with its own gravity water, also, title rights to two very large cattle ranches in Magdalena District, another large tract between Caborca and the Gulf of California, a farm and orchard near Altar, all which would come to us.

The plans for getting reasonable revenue from these lands were, to say the least, quite vague. We had some of it rented for very low amounts, specially the farm near Magdalena, "*La Cotena*": 500 *tercias* (bushels) of wheat per year. The Altar farm paid $300 pesos per year, at that time $150.00. The title rights on El Sasabe ranch, Santa Ana, Arituava and Los Pozos had never been claimed, requiring legal process for partition and distribution. These pending matters in Mexico together with claims of my father's estate against the Mexican government for unpaid salaries made me vacillate about applying for American citizenship. In time, however, we made disposition of the farm lands and the houses. The Mexican claims were assigned to a relative who was in a better position to negotiate for them. He collected a small part of them, $15,000.00 pesos in Bonds of the State of Sonora that were worth only 20 cents on the peso. Part of that had to be given to a government official and the rest was lost in the shuffle.

The large claim against the Federal Government was never cleared up. The man to whom it was assigned was a member of our family. He died and we thought it was best to forget it. When these matters were out of the way, I promptly applied for citizenship to carry out my dream and ambition of years. Soon after I was naturalized I enlisted in The National Guard of Arizona. The commanding officers in Tucson were Col. John H. Martin and Major John F. Black.

I must return to my first day in Tucson.

As soon as I was introduced to the ladies of the house, I found my way to the garden in back of the house. I saw trains and locomotives moving about only two blocks away and ran over to see them closely and find out how they operated. The S.P.R.R. yard with its labyrinth of rails and switches amazed me. It was getting dark, and I returned to the house promising myself to come back and see more of the railroad the next morning. My father had been calling me; I ran through the garden in the dark, and my neck caught a clothes line right under my chin—hard enough to throw me flat on my back. I had a red welt on my throat for several days from that. My father told me when I came in that the family knew that I played the flute and were curious to hear me play. I was hardly in the mood but evading was out of the question. l played Schubert's serenade for them and begged to be excused for that evening. Josefita Vásquez was beginning to take piano lessons at that time although she was then 24 years old. My father bought me a number of piano and flute pieces the next day at Mansfeld's Book Store, all of them very good and some quite beyond my capacity— selections from *Norma, Tancredi, The Barber of Seville, Traviata,* and others. In time we learned parts of them. Later he sent me two fine collections of Mexican and Spanish music for piano. So we soon had a music library.

I only had one day of leisure after my arrival while my father took me around to purchase a few things for me. I was outfitted with a supply of the regulation dark blue heavy flannel shirts for work near the forge, also heavy overalls and heavy work shoes. The second day I went to work as a helper to Mr. Vásquez.

I was not altogether green. My experience of a few weeks in Don Manuel Martínez's shop at Magdalena served me in hand. There is little to tell about the work. It meant 10 hours a day of helping in the blacksmith forge: blowing a bellows, swinging a ten pound sledge, hard grinding, filing carriage forgings; taking wagons apart for repairs and putting parts together; and observing how the iron and steel were shaped by hammering red hot iron, welding, tempering and fitting, drilling, cutting threads, and finishing. The shop life was interesting, but the same one day as the next. I had three years of that without any pay. The 4th year I was paid $8.00 per week and my board and room—the 5th year, $12.00 per week and room and board.

Tío Adolfo Vásquez was getting along in years, about 35, and had not yet married. He decided to look around, and while his mind was absorbed in this, he neglected his business very much. Sometimes he would stay away for a month at a time. This gave me a chance to run the shop and take care of all the details. By that time I was getting efficient in my trade and ambitious to try different work, heavier machine forging in Railroad shops, etc. So we will forget the carriage trade . . . and tell about the life at home and about the town.

My father wanted Mr. Dalton to arrange for me to attend night school or have private lessons at night principally in accounting, English, and music. Mr. Dalton said that he would be glad to teach me himself and also give me classes in French and said that in music he would see that I would not neglect practicing, would have me join a local band and practice with me. He had learned to play cornet and also could play some on the flute. He had a good cornet and played with this band twice a week in the evening for the pleasure of it. He also had an old French flute which I soon discovered was a very fine one.

I had finished the English Ollendorf in school before I left Altar and could read and write English fairly well, but my night lessons with Mr. Dalton helped me a lot. I found great difficulty with the pronunciation of French, and my father advised me to drop it. The musical practices did not last long. As a matter of fact, Mr. Dalton's musical education had been limited, and he decided that he could not help me very much in that. However, he took me to the band room and introduced me to Mr. Katz, the director. Mr. Katz was glad to have me as they needed a piccolo player. The first time the band played, I thought that the roof of the room would blow off. They were all beginners and their playing was not at all inspiring. So I dropped out.

My evenings at home were all occupied with my lessons, practicing my flute, writing music, and reading for my Tía Chona. My father sent me several good books, and Mr. Dalton also had a good number of them. During those years, I read many Dumas works in Spanish for Tía Chona, many of Pérez Escrich, Victor Hugo, Jules Verne, and many others. Tía Chona would sit up many times until midnight listening until I would get too sleepy to read clearly.

I would call sometimes on my mother's aunt, Mrs. Pedro Aguirre, Tía Chatita, a very lovely old lady, my grandfather's sister. Her daughter Beatríz was then about 20 years old, and very lovely. Her older sister, Margarita, had lost her husband the year before and was living with her mother. They were all very fine to me and it was a pleasure to call on them. These Aguirre girls gave me my first lesson in dancing. However, I never took very much to dancing. One night I went to Levin's Park, a beer park . . . . I found that my old music teacher Don

Lazaro Valencia and his small orchestra had been engaged to play at the park for the season. When Don Lazaro saw me he fell over my neck and nothing would do but for me to play the flute parts with the orchestra. Their flute player was glad to be relieved while I took his place. Before I knew it, it was 12 o'clock. Next morning Tía Chona had to know where I had been and I was told to stay away from the Park.

In the shop of Dalton and Vásquez where I was serving my time there were four young men with whom I naturally made friends although they were all several years older than I— Manuel Zúñiga, a blacksmith helper whose father Captain Bernardo Zúñiga had been a soldier under my father during the French invasion of Mexico; his uncle, Don Maximo Zúñiga, who had also been one of my father's soldiers, had a barber shop on Meyer Street only a few doors south of our carriage shop. The old print by my bed of the boy looking at his sweetheart with adoring eyes while the dog looks at both was one of Don Maximo's art pictures in the barber shop. He knew that I admired this print very much and when he closed his shop several years later he gave it to me. I know it is a cheap picture, but I love it now as I loved it then when I was 14 or 15 years old and used to go to Don Maximo Zúñiga's barber shop to have my hair cut and also to hear him tell the episodes, true or otherwise, of the time he was a soldier in Mexico before I was born. He told me many things about my father's military life that I had never heard before.

The other three shop mates were: Santos Aros, a young

painter, who could play the guitar by ear (Santos Aros taught me the position of all the major and relative minor chords on the guitar); Frank O'Neil, a young Irishman, was a horseshoer, quite a romantic fellow and full of fun. The other one was Carlos Gastelum, also a painter full of fun, a dudish dresser, good dancer and quite a fighter. However, he loved to be considered artistic and many other things that he was not. Carlos Gastelum was the only one of the four that lived to be an old man. He left two or three sons that look very much like him, but seem more intelligent, one of them, a butcher at the Public Market and the other a hardware clerk at Steinfeld's [Department Store]. As I go along I will recall funny episodes connected with Santos Aros, Manuel Zúñiga, Frank O'Neil, and Carlos Gastelum.

Maximo Zúñiga had a way to exploit his young friends. He took a liking to a gold watch that my brother Henry had given me in trade for a silver one which had a fine movement. Zúñiga would admire my gold watch and tell me to let him know if I ever wanted to sell it. It was not long before I needed a few dollars and offered my watch for sale. Zúñiga worked on me until he traded his own silver watch, which was supposed to be very special with an excellent movement, for my gold watch. He gave me $15 to boot. This wonderful silver watch did not keep good time and in a few weeks ceased to run. I sold it to one of the shop boys for $10. Ten years later a friend of mine showed me a fine gold watch on which he had loaned Zúñiga $100. It was my old one for which I only got $25.

Zúñiga tricked me also into buying from him an old Singer sewing machine for $35 to give it to my sister, Maggie, but at another time he did not fare so well. He had an antique barber chair, hand carved, with beautiful swan heads in the side arms. The wood was mahogany but the years of use had made it look dirty. He offered me $5 if I would clean, repolish it and varnish it. It was a tedious job to scrape the old varnish from all the carving. It took several nights from 7 P.M. to 9 and 10 [P.M.]. I did a good job of cleaning and polishing, and if the chair had been rubbed with oil or a light quick-drying varnish it would have looked fine, but Zúñiga insisted on the best-wearing English Valentine body varnish. He had heard us say around the carriage shop that this particular brand of varnish was the finest for finish and long life. He did not know, neither did I, that it required a specially prepared surface to take it. So I talked our painter out of a pint of this fine varnish and I made Mr. Zúñiga very happy by applying it to this chair. It looked gorgeous, but when it failed to harden after 24 hours he refused to pay me the $5. I hoped and prayed for the varnish to dry up for several days. It never did, so I lost my $5, and Zúñiga never could use his beautifully carved mahogany chair. Attempting to clean that varnish was something that no one cared to undertake. He agreed that it was a mutual mistake and we both took our loss.

Maximo Zúñiga was not only a barber, he was the neighborhood wit, practical joker, self-appointed celebrator of the Mexican national days and he also used to extract teeth, and sometimes he would pull out the wrong ones.

Soon after I had started to work I had an opportunity to see, what was called here, a western picnic. Tío Adolfo and two or three of his friends were in charge. The invited guests were fifty or more families. They drove to a place under the cottonwoods at the Rillito River near Fort Lowell. There was a steer butchered, large wood fires made, and the men all had long sticks with sharp points to stick pieces of meat and broil them over the live coals. They had other good things to eat, and beer and wine for everybody. Two Italian musicians that played the violin and the harp furnished fine music for dancing on large canvas. These Italians were Juan and Pancho Pascalli. I got well acquainted with them. Returning to town after a very fine day we had a hard time managing Jacob Martin, a friend of the Vásquez and Dalton families. Martin was a good hearted, easy going, likeable young man until he would take a few drinks. Even a few glasses of beer would make him lose his head and become violent and entirely a different person.

I was invited to two other picnics after that, one to the ranch of Don Emilio Carrillo near Tanque Verde, and another one to Agua Caliente. These places we can now reach in one short hour by automobile. At that time it would take several hours from town by horses.

My social life covering these years consisted mainly of gatherings with some of the shop boys until I made a few acquaintances on account of my music. I was naturally shy and did not meet any young women. I would play with different groups of musicians at different times for the pleasure of it.

My first 16th of September (Mexican Independence Day) 1882 in Tucson was celebrated with a great public feast. They had a number of fine floats in the parade, and a troupe of boys had been uniformed and drilled to act as a guard of honor to the queen and her court. I was a private in that troupe. The parade marched to Levin's Park where the annual fiesta of St. Agustín was in full sway. This feast (honoring the patron saint of Tucson) started on the 28th of August and lasted for a month. The guard of honor was formed in a square along the back of both sides of the stage. The queen of the celebration and her maids of honor occupied the center and the members of the *Junta Patriótica* (the executive committee) and the speakers sat on the sides. The official speaker of the evening was to be Don Vicente Lomelí, the Mexican consul, a highly cultured gentleman who had just arrived from Mexico City. Everyone was anticipating a Spanish masterpiece as he came with the reputation of a fine orator. The first musical numbers in the program were given and when Sr. Lomelí did not appear, his secretary stepped forward and in a few words told the waiting audience that the Hon. Consul was indisposed and begged the audience to excuse him. This left the Junta without a speaker, and in a rather embarrassing situation.

This same barber, Maximo Zúñiga, who was a member of the Junta on the stage, went to the Chairman and pointing to me told him that he knew I had prepared a speech to deliver it at the end of the program when it was the custom to invite voluntary speakers. I had prepared a patriotic speech, more for the fun of it than expecting to have a chance to use it. I had recited it to Zúñiga in the barber shop when there was no one else around and he had liked it. So the President of the Junta pulled me out of the ranks and announced to the audience that I would speak. I am sure that I must have been scared stiff, but I knew my piece and I delivered it so that every one would be sure to hear it. It evidently made a hit at least with a good part of the crowd. Before we left the stage and after the regulation *abrazos* [hugs] of congratulation someone brought me an invitation to a champagne supper. Before I could decide what to do I was pulled through the mob into one of the restaurants (*fondas*) of the fiesta and here were eight or more women and men standing around a table loaded with food and bottles. I was to be the guest of honor, a boy of 15 years old.

I don't remember how I acted. I do remember that I did not like the champagne and drank water. The next day I received by a messenger boy a very nice letter and a silver eagle cut out of a Mexican peso. Don Miguel Roca, the father of our well known citizen, City Councilman and personal friend, Lautaro Roca, had sent me the letter and the eagle in appreciation of my speech. Don Miguel Roca was a native of Chile but was then a merchant and a prominent citizen of Tucson. His family was socially prominent and leaders among the best people at that time. Of his daughters we still have with us Mrs. Ben Heney and Mrs. George Smalley. I remember particularly that Mrs. Ben Heney, Erminia Roca, was an accomplished pianist and an attractive girl.

After this celebration and my unexpected introduction I

met a good many people and made some very dear friends. However, I suffered much embarrassment at times on account of my position of a simple apprentice in a shop where it was necessary to wear overalls and go around with face and hands full of grease and coal soot. I had to go from my work in my working clothes and some of my men acquaintances did not care to recognize me without a white collar. There were exceptions, however, and I have in mind one lady who never failed to give me a most cordial greeting no matter how grimy my face or my clothes. That was Mrs. A. V. Grosetta, Warren Grosetta's mother. I became acquainted with A. V. Grosetta and his young wife soon after they were married on account of our mutual love of music. She played the piano. Mr. Grosetta played clarinet and I played the flute. The boys at the R.R. shop had organized a band sponsored by Master Mechanic Bonner, and A. V. Grosetta was the leader. I joined it and played a baritone more than a piccolo, so I took up the baritone and played that until that band was disbanded.

On the following 16th of September, 1883, I had charge of the chorus girls and boys to sing the National Mexican Hymn. We needed a good tenor and someone remembered that a Spaniard, whom everybody liked, by the name of Rufino Vélez had a very good tenor voice. I had seen Rufino Vélez once or twice. He was a short man from the waist down. His body was of normal size, with very powerful short arms, and he always cropped his hair short. He walked with a swing, a large cigar in his mouth and no hat. For a better idea of his body: his trousers had to be made to order 42" waist and 22" long. His tailors would refuse to believe these dimensions before checking them two or three times. When he sat in an ordinary chair, his head and shoulders were on a level with those of any large man but his feet would not reach the floor.

He came to our rehearsal and his voice, so large and of such beautiful quality, made us all stare at him in wonder. He did not know a single note and could only carry a melody if someone else would sing or play along with him. I had to coach him and sing along with him in a soft voice so that his own wonderful voice could be heard pure. We had a lot of fun and became warm friends. We called each other *compañero* and he proved to be the best chum and friend I ever had in this world. He was a man around 30 years old and I was only 16. . . .

[Rufino] was a Vizcaino, Vasco from Balmaceda near Bilbao [in Spain]. His father was a fisherman and also the official musician at Balmaceda. He played a *silvo* (a small flageolet with 3 holes and a tamborin). Rufino left Spain when 14 years old. He was sent to an uncle who had a store in Mazatlán, Mexico. It took his ship, an English sailing bark, six months from Liverpool around Cape Horn to Mazatlán. He worked for his uncle for six years, saved his money, and he and a young friend named Durazo put their savings together, bought a load of Guadalajara wear and other trinkets, chartered a small schooner and sailed with their stock to Puerto Libertad where they loaded their wares on a 10-mule wagon and headed for Altar through the desert. This happened in the year of 1875 about the time we were to leave for Guaymas. I remember when all the boys in Altar were blowing Guadalajara ware whistles purchased from the new store of Durazo and Vélez. Of course I do not remember Rufino at that time.

He was in Altar during the Serna revolution. One day the soldiers placed him on a bareback horse and led him into the foothills to demand a contribution of $400 or his life. He gave the officer a piece of his mind in warm Spanish vernacular for making him ride a bareback horse and they returned to Altar to get the $400.

He sold his half interest in the store to his partner Durazo and stayed in Altar having a good time, dancing and singing until the money was all gone. He came to Tucson, worked as a clerk for Lord and Williams, saved his money again and in time he opened a dry goods store with José Rebeil. Their main sales were made to Altar merchants who in those days used to transport their purchases in bundles covered in heavy white duck sewed tight to make them waterproof. They would use two-and-a-half yards of canvas for each bundle and would sell the canvas for sleeping cots. The merchants would charge 50 cents for the labor of making each bundle. Rufino was an expert at that and many days he would make twenty or more bundles. The bundles were made up to weigh about 50 pounds so that a man on horseback could carry two of them on his horse. All these bundles of dry goods, shoes and all kinds of goods were smuggled across the Mexican line by expert horsemen. They had good horses, knew the trails away from the traveled roads, and were hard to catch by the Mexican custom house guards.

A Tucson merchant named Isidor Myers sold a good number of bundles to some Mexican smugglers and in place of making up the bundles with the new goods for which the Mexican smugglers had paid their cash, Isidor made some easy money by filling up the bundles with rags, old shoes, and old clothes; he then sent word to the Mexican custom house at Sasabe that these smugglers were to leave Tucson on a certain day and cross the border the following night. The guards set a trap and caught the smugglers with the bundles full of trash. Myers paid plenty for this trick. He did not only lose all the smugglers' trade, but, for fear that some of them would kill him, he sold his store and left Tucson and did not come back until many years later.

The smugglers were considered legitimate traders. Most of them were men of great courage and the guards were not always anxious to encounter them. They had fine horses, good arms and many friends among the ranchers. One of the outstanding smugglers was Damacio García. Several of his sons and descendants are living on the old ranch near Sasabe and in Arivaca.

The firm of Vélez and Rebeil closed their store about 1882 soon after I came to Tucson. Rufino Vélez continued to handle purchases for Altar merchants on commission. He also kept the books and handled the stage lines for Don Mariano

Samaniego, who operated U. S. Mail and passenger lines from Tucson to Arivaca, Oro Blanco, Quijotoa, and Mammoth. It was then that I became acquainted with Rufino and our friendship lasted until he died in 1906.

Mr. Dalton decided that he could do better by taking government contracts and farming, and discontinued his connection with Mr. Vásquez in the carriage shop about 1884. Mr. Vásquez gave me the additional job of keeping the books for the shop. I knew very little about this, but by following the single entry method that Mr. Dalton had used and with an occasional aid from Mr. Dalton and the help of a bookkeeping manual that my father gave me, I managed to get by.

The work in the shop was not as steady after Mr. Dalton left and when Mr. Vásquez had to go out we had more time for playing. Frank O'Neil, the horseshoer, furnished the reason for sports. He loved to start contests of all kinds with us, wrestling, jumping, lifting weights and sparring without boxing gloves and using the fingers only for face slapping. One time we used red paint on the fingers to be sure that the hits would be marked. Frank O'Neil's face was all spotted with red paint. As a rule, he would lose most of the contests.

He made a bet with us that the *"Star Spangled Banner"* was more melodic music than the Mexican National Hymn. I was to whistle the Mexican Hymn and he was to whistle the "Star Spangled Banner." The rest of the shop boys were to be the judges. I whistled my hymn and, before starting the Star Spangled Banner, Frank decided that he could not whistle as well as I and asked me to whistle his piece. I started it terribly out of tune to burlesque the music. Frank was so enraged when he realized my trick that he could not talk. He grabbed a wagon spoke and started for me. I jumped out of his way and ran. The judges were all laughing, and when O'Neil found that he could not reach me after running after me around the shop yard until he got out of wind, he threw the spoke at me and sat down to cuss. We all had a good laugh and paid no attention to his raging.

Frank O'Neil had a fine setter dog that could do tricks and he loved to show him off. He would give the dog a dollar to hold in his mouth and dare any of us to take it away from him. One day he did not have a silver coin and used a $5.00 gold coin for the trick. The dog took the $5.00 piece, looked at Frank as if asking for instructions and swallowed the gold. Frank lost his head, gave the poor dog a whipping, and chained him to a wagon out in the shop yard. Every time that any of us boys would go out to the yard Frank would drop his horse shoeing and run out to see if the dog had expelled the $5.00. We had no end of fun with him while the dog kept the gold in his stomach. He finally recovered it by giving the dog an emetic.

Another time we all walked to Warner's Lake in the evening for a swim. Warner's Lake was about 40 acres of water at the south foot of A Mountain (Sentinel Peak). Frank O'Neil and his dog came along with us. We all got into the water excepting O'Neil. He got into a small canoe with the dog and said he would paddle around the lake while we swam. It was quite dark, and when we were all out and ready to dress, O'Neil was no where to be seen. We called him, shouting as loud as we could and would get no answer. Fearing that something could have happened to him we swam toward the middle of the lake, and there was Frank lying face down on the canoe full of water without any clothes and the dog was trying to climb over his back. We pulled him out and when we lighted some matches we found that the dog had scratched his face and his body severely in several places.

He had taken his clothes off while in the water, thinking that he could hang on to the canoe as he could not swim, and while he attempted to do this with the dog jumping around, the canoe capsized and all his clothes, his hat and his shoes went to the bottom of the lake. He tried to climb on the canoe and finally succeeded in turning it over, but it was full of water. We had a good laugh at him while trying to outfit him with an undershirt and a pair of underdrawers from one of the boys. They were several sizes too small for him. He had to walk barefooted into town with us. He told us that he had quite a lot of money in his trousers. Manuel Zúñiga and I went to the lake the following Sunday to dive for the trousers. We found them, but there was only $1.75 in silver in the pockets. We also found his pocket knife and keys. We gave him back the trousers, the keys and the knife, and Manuel and I divided the dollar and seventy five cents.

Before Warner's Lake was destroyed by Santa Cruz River floods I made a flat bottom skiff of redwood boards. I used oakum in the seams and painted the entire outside with a mixture of pitch and tallow, as I had seen the boat makers do at La Paz. Manuel Zúñiga and I carried this little boat on our heads from the shop to the lake. It was not an easy job. I thought it would hold us both, but when we launched it and got into it, it nearly swamped. We could only use it one of us at a time. I made a pair of oars and also forged a pair of oar locks. I had a lot of fun with it until one Sunday afternoon when I was rowing in the lake I got careless and turned over. I had my best Sunday clothes and ruined them while I climbed over the boat's bottom. I had put too much tallow in the pitch and it had never dried.

Warner's Lake was the popular place for the boys and girls of the town to gather on Sundays, so I had a good audience when I climbed out of the water with my Sunday suit all wet and full of black pitch. I never used the boat again. Many years after the dam collapsed and the lake was dried up, my little boat used to lie by the side of the road around the A Mountain.

Before the dam that formed Warner's Lake was washed away by tremendous floods of the Santa Cruz, there was no channel in the valley west of Tucson. The water was checked, first at Silver Lake and next at Warner's Lake. Below Warner's Lake there was a short channel through the Carrillo farm and from there the water was taken out in irrigation ditches. In flood times the water would spread over what is now Menlo Park, and the part that is occupied by the E.P. and S.W. [El Paso and Southwestern Railroad] tracks north of Congress

Street was covered with stagnant water for months after a flood. The present channel of the Santa Cruz running west of town was cut by the floods that took the lake dam about 1890 or 1891.

Silver Lake was a beautiful body of clear water about a quarter mile wide and a half mile long. It was started by Jimmy Lee to operate a flour mill by water power. Some years later Silver Lake was acquired by Maish and Driscoll. A two story frame building was built on the west bank of the lake in 1883. Here they had a boat house, a number of row boats to rent, fishing poles and tackle, also a bar and restaurant and a dance hall. It was quite a resort. I used to walk the four or five miles from town to Silver Lake once in a while on Sundays and expend my 50 cents for an hour on a row boat. Later when I started to get pay for my work, Rufino Vélez and I would hire a buggy from the livery stables and go to Silver Lake for a swim. Rufino was a very good swimmer. One day we cut a watermelon from a melon patch near the lake. The Chinese owner saw us and turned his dog loose on us. I never forget Rufino's figure running for dear life with the water-melon and jumping in the lake with it yelling and laughing at the top of his lungs.

Manuel Zúñiga and I also made a velocipede on Sundays. The wheels were made of wood, the tall one like a buggy wheel. The frame and pedals were made of iron. I would try to ride it, and something about it would break. After remodel-ing it two or three times, the tall wheel went to pieces during a try out and we abandoned it. We would also make iron benches for Tía Chona's garden and ornamented bookshelves and corner tables for bric a brac. All these things had to be made on Sundays or during the noon hour.

Tía Chona treated me like her own son, and I learned to love her. There was nothing I would not do for her. She would tell me about her early life in Altar. Her father had studied for the priesthood, knew something about medicine, and finally decided to marry and learn the trade of jeweler and goldsmith. He knew an Indian who would come to town from time to time with gold nuggets and pieces of quartz encrusted with streaks of pure gold. He liked Mr. Suastegui and offered to take him to the place where the gold was. They started out on horseback, and when the Indian showed him the hill from where he got the gold, a few miles away, they were surprised by a band of Papago Indians and a volley of arrows. The Indian friend was killed, and Mr. Suastegui's life was saved by one of the Papagos who recognized him as a man who had befriended and cured him at one time. This same Indian took him back to Altar. Mr. Suastegui had several arrow wounds from which he never recovered entirely. He described, as well as he could remember, the location where the Indians had attacked him and the hill where the gold was supposed to be. Some of his relatives tried to find the place and others have looked for it in the vicinity of Quitobac, but so far no one has found the gold.

Tía Chona would also tell me about her trip from Altar to Los Angeles in a covered wagon with her two small daughters and son Adolfo Vásquez, Jesusita, who became Mrs. Dalton, and Josefita, who was never married; their arrival at Los Angeles when Los Angeles was a small town populated principally by Spanish pioneer families; [and] how she became acquainted with Mrs. Henry Dalton and her friends.

About the last year of my apprenticeship, I was called home when one of my little brothers died from diphtheria and another one, the youngest, was scalded by a pitcher of boiling milk that he pulled down over his body from a table in the kitchen. His name was Armando, the baby of the family, about three years old. He only lived a few days. The other boy, Rodolfo, was 5 years old and my father's pet. His death nearly killed my father. When I arrived home, I saw the picture of grief was terrible. My brother Joe, who was about seven years old, was still in bed after a bad case of diphtheria. My father's health was poor and his spirit badly broken up. He was thinking of resigning his position with the Railroad Co. on account of his failing health. My visit with him for a few days made him feel better.

We had a farm at Altar rented for a nominal amount, and my father thought that perhaps I could find someone to buy it if I would go to Altar and see how the place was and offer it to some of the people we knew there able to pay for it. It was decided that I should go. My father sent brother Dick to a friend of his, a Mr. Loaiza, who had a good saddle horse not being used, to tell him that he would like to borrow the horse for a trip I was to make to Altar two days later. Dick took the message (verbally), but instead of delivering it as it was given to him, he borrowed the horse and saddle to have a ride himself, took it back and put it in the stable at night and thought that the horse would be there when he would call again to get it for my trip. The evening before I was to start, my father told Dick to go and get the horse so I could have it in our own stable for my early morning start.

When Dick called for the horse, Mr. Loaiza had sent it to his ranch. As Dick had used the horse himself for a good ride and returned it to Mr. Loaiza's stable he understood that my father had used the horse and did not need it any more. Dick had failed to deliver the right message.

When my father scolded him, Dick said that he could get another horse from a friend and, sure enough, when I went to our stable to saddle the horse at 4 A.M. for an early start, I found it was a mare with a two months old colt. I saddled the mare anyway and started out with the colt following but found it was next to impossible to make the colt follow. At San Lorenzo, a few miles out of Magdalena, I hired a horse from a farmer and left the mare and colt for him to return to its owner. I made the trip from Magdalena to Altar, 75 leagues, in one day. The horse was good. I was young, 16 years, and not very heavy and galloped most of the way.

I had no luck in selling the farm. No buyers for it. After four days I started back to Magdalena. This time I took it easy and stopped at Ocuca for the night. The Ocuca Ranch is noted for its beautiful forests of heavy mesquite trees and some wonderful valleys which at that time, the month of August, were covered with green grass two feet high. It had rained hard in the afternoon going from Altar to Ocuca and all the country looked grand. This was my third trip through the Ocuca, and I enjoyed it immensely, riding at the sunrise when cattle and horses were frolicking over the green plains. Five years before I had come through the same road with Antonio Redondo who was married to my half sister, Maggie. Antonio drove a fine team of grays, one of them quite green to his four passenger road wagon, from Altar to Imuris. Antonio was suffering from partial paralysis and I went with him to help him. He had to take a glass of egg nog after bathing in the mineral hot springs near Imuris every day, and it was my job to prepare it for him.

We had stopped two days at El Ocuca ranch and this gave me a chance to see the *ordeñas* [a place where cows are milked], about 100 milk cows for making *quesadillas* and cheese, also the branding of the young colts, and the bonfires around which the vaqueros gathered at night to sing and tell yarns. The Ocuca was the home of the original Redondo[7] from Spain and had been a hotbed for the Apache Indians for many years.

On the way to Magdalena our young horse caught the line under the tail and started to run. I jumped out of the wagon and ran in front of the team to stop them as they were going in a circle while Antonio could only pull on the free line of the other horse. He shouted to me to get out of the horses' way, fearing that they would run over me, but before I knew it I was hanging onto the bridle of the new horse and the team had stopped.

We stayed several days at Imuris. While Antonio would bathe in the hot spring, I would prepare an egg nog with two eggs and a good portion of brandy for him to take as soon as he would come out of the water. That was our routine every day excepting one day when Don Francisco Quiroga invited us to his ranch a few miles from Imuris. He was the brother of my father's first wife, Doña Chonita Quiroga. My two half sisters, Maggie and Chonita, had taught me to call an oil painting of their mother which hung in our home, "Mama Chonita."

The Quirogas were not related to my own mother but treated her and us children as their own relatives. We had been stopping at Imuris in the home of my half brother, Henry. Tío Francisco Quiroga had ridden a fine saddle horse when he came over to invite us to visit his hacienda; and in order to ride with Antonio and Henry in the spring wagon I was given his saddle horse to ride along with them. I had to gallop to keep up with the horses pulling the road wagon, and before I realized it my horse was heated and started on a run through the forest. I could not hold him, so I had to dodge trees and brush until the horse started to lose his wind and respond to my pull on the bridle.

The day we were hitching the horses to return to Altar the new horse balked while the neck yoke straps were being fastened, causing the end of the pole to drag on the ground. It did not take long for the wagon to upset. The pole sweep was broken, and all the top standards also broke off. The local blacksmith took over a week to hammer old tires by hand to make patching plates to fasten the top standards in place. He had to cut green ash branches to bend a sweep for the pole. Two or three were spoiled before he could make one. To me all these operations were very entertaining.

On our return trip we stopped another two days at El Ocuca. I had my fill once more of delicious warm milk and foam right out of the cows. I also tried to rope a small colt in the corrals. In fact I did rope it, but I got a good fall and lost the rope. One of the *vaqueros* had to recover it. I learned that a horse colt a few months old takes a grown man who knows how to hold it, and I did not try any more colt-roping at that time.

I can never forget the religious celebrations that Father Suastegui and the good people of Altar used to have in those days. Around Christmas time they would have a pageant to show some of the historical events before the coming of the Saviour: A young girl representing Mary, a young girl dressed as an angel announcing to Mary the conception of the Christ Child, then the trek of Joseph and Mary to Bethlehem, the Nativity, the coming of the three wise kings following the star of Bethlehem. The star looked real, traveling along a wire. All these, to me, very beautiful and impressive tableaux remain fresh in my memory.

During Holy Week they also had tableaux and a pageant showing the way of the Cross. In the court yard of the church there would be a forest of olives where the Christ would be arrested by the soldiers of Pilatus; while all this was going on, no church bells would be heard. The calls were made by *matracas* (a board with two iron rings that boys would carry along the streets of the town, shaking them and making a noise like drumming on a board with metal paddles). This pageant would end on Saturday at the resurrection when all the bells would resume their pealing. The church choir would sing Gloria in Excelsis and the children would empty baskets of flowers into the air. The Judas would be burned in effigy, and the whole town would rejoice.

Some of the pagan half-Indian religious pageants held by the Yaqui Indians about this time are no doubt a crude imitation of what the Spanish people did in Mexico in early times.[8]

I knew that my father was not going to be able to work for long and felt that it would be up to me to take care of him, my mother and sister, and my two young brothers. I returned to Tucson and my job of $8.00 per week and my board and room. I would manage to send my mother $20.00 every month from that as my personal expenses were very small. The fifth year when I was getting $12.00 per week and board and room I would send my mother $30.00 per month.

During these years of 1886 and 1887 my position at Tía Chona's home had changed. While I was a boy of 18 and 19 years I was treated like a man and with a great kindness and consideration. Mr. Dalton and his family had moved to a farm house that he had leased, near the A Mountain, from Don Leopoldo Carrillo. Part of this home still stands across the road from the ruins of the old adobe mission [the *visita* of San Agustín del Tucson].[9] I used to walk out to this place frequently in the evenings to see Mrs. Dalton and the children, all of whom I loved dearly. My wife Lupe was then a little girl of 1-1/2 years. On Sunday morning I would go early and help Mrs. Dalton come into town to church, and many times I carried Lupita in my arms all the way.

The unmarried daughter of Tía Chona, Josefita, called "Vía" by the Dalton children, was taking piano lessons all the time and making some progress. I was called regularly to help her to read her music and practice flute and piano music. She was entirely a different type from her sister, Mrs. Dalton, both in looks and disposition. Mrs. Dalton was beautiful and sweet while Josefita was short, inclined to be stout, rather determined in manner and at times of violent temper. However, she had been very carefully trained by her mother. In Tía Chona's traditional Spanish custom, her daughters had never been permitted to go any place without a chaperon or to meet young men, go to dances or parties unless their mother would take them. Josefita had never attended a dance or met any young men.

Tía Chona, poor soul, in her motherly affection for me encouraged my association with her daughter. I was asked to take her to the theatre and to drive her out in the evenings and Sundays as often as Tío Adolfo's buggy and horse were available. She showed me more regard than she had ever had for any one, and it was perhaps the natural thing for me to develop an affection for her, particularly as I had no time or opportunity to see or associate with other girls. She was a good girl with all her difficult disposition and could have made a good wife to a man fifteen years older than I was. I was eighteen and she was about twenty nine.

It was a great mistake of my Tía Chona to have ever entertained the idea that I might become her son-in-law, and when I realized it, my situation became extremely difficult. I never dreamed of getting married for many years. I knew that I would have all I could do to support my parents and brothers, and when the possibility of my friendship for Josefita was first suggested to me as being more serious than I had ever considered it, I felt as if my world was coming to its end. I did not have the courage to oppose the well expressed wishes of Tía Chona and Josefita that I should think seriously of getting married. In that I made a great mistake. I should have not only said as I did say that I did not feel I had a right to marry at my age, without any funds and with my own parents and small brothers and sister depending on me for their support, but that I had no idea of sacrificing my entire life to show my gratitude to Tía Chona for her care and kindness to me while I was learning my trade.

Many young men will play along with a girl and become engaged to her against their will. They know that they do not love her, that she has nothing to make them happy, and still follow the line of least resistance until they consider themselves duty bound to make her a wife, and in nine cases out of ten [they] wreck not only their own happiness for life, but also the happiness of the poor girl and many times the lives of their children. I believe that the honorable and square thing to do is to break an engagement, even at the last minute in church before the actual wedding, when there is no real love and satisfaction that the marriage is going to be a happy one.

My foolish involuntary engagement to Josefita was finally ended one day after I had to bring my parents to Tucson and provide a place for them to live when my father's health broke down completely. I had moved from Tía Chona's home to a house I had rented for my parents. Neither Tía Chona nor Josefita could say anything about that, but I knew they did not like it.

One day, Josefita had a case of temper because, as she said, she suspected that I was half-hearted and indifferent. She could not control her anger when I said nothing and started to leave the room. This gave me my opportunity. I left and felt as if a mountain had been taken from my back. I felt very sorry for Tía Chona and for realizing that I would lose the love and motherly affection which she had given me for all the years that I had lived in her home. I was also deeply concerned about what Mrs. Dalton would think of me.

Tía Chona waited for me at the morning hour when she knew I would pass by her house on my way to work to tell me how sorry she was for her daughter's outburst of temper and begged me not to stay away from her house on account of it. She told me that as far as she was concerned it had all been a mistake and to forget it. I was touched very deeply for this as

I loved Tía Chona almost as if she had been my own mother. I knew how proud she was and what it was costing her to talk to me in that way, but I also knew that I could never go back to her house.

The first time I saw Mr. Dalton, I spoke to him about this matter, hoping that he would not blame me much. He did not hesitate to tell me that he was glad for my sake and that he and his wife, Mrs. Dalton, whom I also loved dearly, had never approved of it. This was a great relief for me. I called on Mrs. Dalton and she was as gracious to me as ever, but as her sister and Tía Chona were always near her I knew that Mrs. Dalton was embarrassed and I did not see her again for several years.

My limited musical training gave me opportunities to meet people of consequence that otherwise I would not have known at that time. I was invited to join a band, a group of railroad shop men, which had been organized by Master Mechanic Bonner. Mr. Bonner played the trombone, and while he could play very little, he loved it. I became well acquainted with him when he expressed a desire to get a few old melodies like "*Swanee River,*" "*Old Black Joe,*" and others written in easy key for trombone, and I got some music paper and wrote several for him. He was very much pleased and told me that if I ever wanted to work in a railroad shop to come to him and he would give me a place. He also made me a present of a gold pen.

Sometime after that I decided to ask Mr. Bonner for a job in the locomotive blacksmith shop. He told me to come to work as soon as I was ready. I told Tío Vásquez why I had thought it best to leave him. He agreed with me that I was right. He had been unable to pay my wages for several weeks, and after I cleaned up some unfinished work, I reported to the foreman of the railroad shop. This man's name was Charles Miller. He was a splendid mechanic, and it was a great experience for me to work under him.

At that time, all the iron work on locomotives was forged by hand. The blacksmith shop had four forges. Charles Miller's forge did all the heavy work, welding connecting rods when they came in broken, forging piston links, reversing links and welding fractures in locomotive frames, difficult jobs, all of them requiring skill and accuracy. We had a steam hammer, heavy cranes and a great number of heavy tongs, swedges, and stamps for all kinds of work. One day a helper named Palmer swung his twelve pound sledge out of line hitting my own hammer on the upper stroke. It hit me a glancing blow on the side of the head, cutting a long gash. A half inch closer would have cracked my skull.

The few months I worked at locomotive blacksmithing gave me many ideas for handling forgings many times larger and heavier than anything I had ever seen in the carriage shop.

One Sunday while talking to Filiberto Aguirre, a friend of Tío Vásquez, I learned that Tío Vásquez was looking for someone to whom he could sell or lease the shop. Aguirre told me that since I was acquainted with the work, having operated the carriage shop myself for Tío Vásquez for several months, I should take advantage of the opportunity and take the shop myself. At first I thought his suggestion that I would attempt to lease the shop and go into business for myself was preposterous, having neither capital nor experience in business, but the more I thought about it the less impossible it seemed. Tío Vásquez owed me some $50 or $60. I had $150 coming to me in back salary from the Railroad Co. I only owed Tía Chona $30 for board, and since Tío Vásquez had but remnants of material, a few bolts and malleables, I figured that I had enough to purchase these odds and ends from him if he would lease me the shop and tools for a reasonable amount, payable monthly.

When I spoke to him about this he was greatly surprised, but after a few moments he said: "Well, I don't see why you could not run this shop for yourself, since you ran it for me for several months when I was away."

The deal was made and I took my resignation to Charles Miller and Mr. Bonner. They were glad to know I was to start in business for myself and wished me good luck. I took over the old shop where I had learned my trade and worked hard for five years. I was not quite 20 years old. It was the first of November, 1887. The first month I did over $300 of repair work and I felt very much encouraged.

I wrote to my father and asked him to come to Tucson with the family—that I had my own business and felt confident that I could take care of them.

I rented a house . . . . I bought a few chairs, a stove and kitchen utensils, some china, knives and forks, made some tables and cupboards, also some canvas cots, and bought a supply of groceries—flour, lard, coffee, rice, sugar, tea, bacon, beans, macaroni, potatoes, salt, pepper, and some honey, and a few canned goods. When my father and mother came (in 1887) with Dick about 14, Emilia about 12, and Pepe about 7, I had a home where we could all camp and about a month's supply of food. Tía Chona helped me to get the house ready and it was a great day for all of us when the family arrived and we were all together once more. Emilia and Pepe went to school after a few weeks but Dick was assigned to work with me in the shop. He proved very difficult for me to manage and I decided, after consulting with my parents, that it would be better for Dick to learn the machinist trade if I would place him in the railroad shops with Mr. Bonner's help.

Dick had learned to play piano and flute. I had introduced him to the members of the railroad band and he had joined, playing the piccolo. Mr. Bonner knew him and gave him a place as soon as I asked him for it.

Dick could not talk a word of English, but my father and I coached him to learn a few necessary expressions. I gave him a list of the shop tools with the names in English and Spanish, and it did not take him long to learn. In place of going to the machine shop he was placed in the boiler shop. He learned the boilermaker's trade and was paid $2.50 per day from the first day while he was an apprentice.

I needed a woodworker in the carriage shop and wrote to Ildefonso Corrales, who had gone to Guaymas, offering him a bench in the shop. Corrales had worked with me for Tío

Vásquez, and I knew him to be an excellent woodworker and wheelwright. He had known my father when he (my father) was *Prefecto* in Guaymas and bought water from his burros. He also had known my half brother Henry and had always shown great regard for me. When he received my letter, he answered right away saying that he would come at once. He had no money, and since I could not advance him any for living expenses, I fixed up an old stock room in back of the shop that had a fireplace. I got some cooking utensils and a bed for him and cooked his first supper. I made some steaks with gravy, fried potatoes, and coffee for him. We both enjoyed the supper. He had a place to live while he could earn some money.

Corrales and I had been good friends. He was much older than I. He had lived an exciting life in Sonora before coming to Arizona. He had been in several gun fights and had his body all scarred with bullet marks. His father had been a water dealer in Guaymas where he supplied the city with water by leather bags carried by burros. They called these bags *botas*. Each *bota* held about ten gallons of water. They hung on both sides of the burro, the bottom one high enough from the ground to stand a bucket under the valve. The valves were the ends of cows horns stopping a hole about one inch in diameter in the bottom of the *bota*. The end of the horn, about six inches in length, with the large end up would stick point down into the hole in the leather. The pressure of the water would push it tightly in place. To draw the water the bucket would be set under the end of the horn and the horn would be pushed upwards enough to let the water leak into the bucket. When the bucket would fill, the horn would be allowed to fall back into place closing the hole.

Mr. Henry Dalton, my wife's grandfather, was an Englishman who accumulated a lot of valuable lands before California became a part of the United States, and at the time that Tía Chona knew him and his family they lived at Azusa where they had a wonderful hacienda. The holdings of the hacienda, including many of the towns in the foothills district, Glendora, and the Santa Anita ranch which later belonged to Lucky Baldwin, were all the property of Mr. Henry Dalton. His wife, Doña Guadalupe Zamorano, belonged to one of the oldest pioneers that came from Spain. Her ancestors were Argüellos and Zamoranos.[10] They had titles and certificates from the King and played leading parts in the early life of California. Henry Dalton III had a parchment book containing the origin of these people, a great curiosity, engraved by hand and with the original seals and rubrics (signatures) of the King of Spain and the men who ruled at that time.

On account of Tía Chona's description of Los Angeles, Azusa, and the country and the people that she and her children had known, I dreamed of coming some day to this wonderful land. [The dream] was revived by letters from my friend and roommate Henry Dalton who had returned to Los Angeles after working in Tucson for a year. Henry was a brother of Mr. W. A. Dalton. He was about ten years older than I. He was not a mechanic, but quite handy with tools. He and the Dalton family had painted to me a glowing picture of California, and Henry's letter influenced me to try it.

[Thus] in 1888 I decided to go to California and establish myself in Los Angeles in the carriage-making business, believing that Los Angeles would be a much better field to improve in my trade. I sold my shop lease and what material I had on hand, gave my mother enough money to run the house for sixty days, and with $49.00 in my pocket, I undertook the trip. I bought a scalper's ticket and took the train. At Colton, California, Henry Dalton met me and made me stay over to go with him the following morning in the baggage car. He was baggage master in a local S.P. train from Colton to Los Angeles.

It was the first week in May and the country was enchanting to me. I had letters from several friends of Mr. Dalton and had no difficulty in getting a room at a house that was owned by Doña Eloisa Sepulveda. The rent was $2.50 per week. This house is still standing, a two-story frame on lower Main Street almost across the street from the old Mission church at the plaza.[11]

I started to look for a job in the carriage shops, and while I was promised the first opening in two of the leading shops, I had to wait. Los Angeles then had a population of about 40,000 people. 10th Street was the edge of the city, and the heart of the retail business was on Main St. between the Pico House and the Baker block where Spring Street started.

The cable car line was being built on Spring Street. All the street cars then were drawn by horses. An electric line was being built on Second Street as an experiment. The Bradbury block was the first five-story building, and it was shown as a wonderful architectural marvel. The public library was then located on Main St. where the present City Hall is now. I would rest my legs in the reading room almost every day after making the rounds of the shops. Since my capital was so limited I had to live with a 15 cent breakfast and a 25 cent dinner.

I took one trip to Santa Monica on the steam railroad and another trip to San Pedro. My old music teacher was living in San Pedro and I invested 45 cents for a round trip ticket on a Sunday excursion. About half way the brakeman shouted that half the train would go to San Pedro and the other half to Long Beach. I misunderstood and took the wrong car. I had to pay the conductor 20 cents more to go to Long Beach. When I got off I could see the ships in San Pedro. The only building in Long Beach was a livery stable with a hot dog stand. The man running it wanted $5.00 to drive me to San Pedro. Of course, it was impossible.

I started to walk the five miles, and when I ran into the estuary or river I took off all my clothes and carried them in a bundle on my head, but before I made half of the stream, the water came to my neck and I had to go back. About 4:00 P.M. a farm wagon came along the beach. I asked the two men driving it if they were going to San Pedro. They said, no, we are only riding along while the tide is low and will go across the river. They said I could ride with them. Crossing the river the water came over the bottom of the wagon box. I sat on the edge of one side and put my feet on the other side of the box to avoid getting wet. When the wagon stopped I got down on the west side of the bay. Two boys going by in a row boat took me across for fifty cents. When I landed on the other side, the train conductor was shouting all aboard and I barely had time to get on when the last excursion train was moving. My return ticket was good, but I saw neither San Pedro nor my old music teacher, Don Lazaro Valencia.

Henry Dalton invited me to visit his mother at their Azusa home. I found it a most interesting place. Henry's mother, Mrs. Dalton (Doña Guadalupe), had been a widow for four years. Mr. Dalton had lost practically all his lands and fortune through years of litigation with squatters who had questioned the Spanish titles to his lands, and also through unfortunate deals in business. At one time Mr. Henry Dalton had loaned a half million pesos to the Mexican government. He would never change his English citizenship and perhaps this had something to do with his difficulties in proving the validity of his land titles. Mrs. Dalton was still vigorous when I knew her. She was a very interesting and remarkable lady. Three of her sons, Henry, Valentín, and Joseph were living with her at the old Azusa homestead. [There were] also Valentín's wife, and the orphaned children of the oldest daughter, Louisa [Luisa], and her husband, Louis [Luis] Wolfskill.[12] The little girl, Isabel, was about 4 years, Julian about 5, and Herbert about 7, all beautiful children. I had my flute with me and played for them simple tunes that they enjoyed. Mrs. Dalton would ask me to play some of the waltzes and polkas that she knew and that I could remember. My visit of a week at Azusa was a delight.

In Los Angeles I also met and had dinner one evening with Mrs. Cardwell, "Soyla" Dalton. Her husband, William Cardwell, was secretary of Senator Stephen White, a smart man but of peculiar ways, always faking and having fun teasing everybody. At Mr. Cardwell's home I met a sister of Doña Guadalupe Dalton, Mrs. Eulalia Estudillo, and her young daughter, a rather pretty girl.

There was a troupe of *Zarzuela* artists in Los Angeles at the time that I had known in Tucson and had enjoyed there a season of *Zarzuelas* (comic operas)—*"La Mascota"* [The Mascot], *"Oliveta,"* *"La Gallina Ciega,"* *"Las Campanas de Carreón"* (Chimes of Normandy), and others. The impresarios were Spaniards Villaseñor y Urena. Urena was the pianist and director. Mercedes Villaseñor was the leading soprano, a very charming girl and enchanting Betina in *The Mascot.* They had a very fine musician with them. His name was Aranda. He had made a great success as a baritone soloist.

The first thing that happened to me was to meet the maestro at the home of the Santa Cruz family for whom I had letters of introduction. He told me of their bad luck in not being able to find theatres where they could play. Next I met Aranda, and he stuck to me like a leech. When I went to Azusa I left him, and when I returned they must have left because I did not hear about them any more.

An old friend of our family, Don Chano Ramírez, came to me one day and told me that my father was very low and wanted me to come back to Tucson. My dream had been to get a job in Los Angeles and then bring my father and mother and all the family here, but since I was having no luck in finding work at my trade, I was afraid that I would get into trouble to live here myself and help my mother in Tucson. A letter came saying that the man to whom I had sold my shop lease had discovered that he was not equal to the demands of the trade and was anxious to sell out at some loss. I decided that I should go back and wrote to my chum, Rufino Vélez, to buy the shop back for me. I had paid my way from Tucson to Los Angeles and lived there for a month without adding anything to my $49.00. I had $12.00 left. Henry Dalton got a pass for me from Los Angeles to Yuma, and from Yuma to Tucson I bought a ticket for $12.85 after borrowing $1.00 from a man that I knew. When I arrived home in Tucson, I found that my mother had only a $5.00 gold coin. Brother Dick had been paid $150.00 for two months R.R. wages but had used it all himself to buy clothes, shoes, etc.

I had left a few accounts due me for collection with my friend Rufino Vélez, and fortunately he had collected some of them. I started to work right away in the old shop where they had several jobs waiting for me.

My father was really failing very fast and died seven months later [in 1889] after much suffering. I had been up all night with him and as soon as daylight came I went to the stage office that my friend Rufino Vélez would open very early to dispatch the stages belonging to Mr. Mariano Samaniego. I had no funds to pay my father's funeral expenses and thought of Mr. Samaniego as a person from whom I might borrow $200.00. I knew him quite well since I would repair his stage coaches and buckboards for him when the repairs were needed. He happened to be up at 5 A.M. in Rufino's office, and when I told him that my father had died and asked him for the loan of $200.00 he gave it to me. I must say here that it took me three years to pay this loan plus 2 per cent per month interest, the usual interest rate at that time.

Rufino took charge of all the arrangements for my father's funeral and made it with the $200.00 borrowed. A few weeks later, Rufino came to my shop and handed me a fist full with fifteen 20 dollar gold pieces, $300.00. I asked him what it was for and he said: "I know that you are buying your material from hand to mouth and paying outrageous prices for it. Use this $300.00 to get a supply from jobbers in the East and do not worry about the time it will take you to pay it back."

I had been paying the local material suppliers $3.00 for a wagon reach, 50 cents for a 2 inch wagon spoke and all other material at similar prices. I had price lists from St. Louis and Chicago houses—2" x 4" oak reaches 10 feet long, 35 cents— 2 inch spokes oak select, 15 cents, etc. The local R.R. freight was high but after adding the weight I saved over one half from what I had been paying. This gave me a real boost and helped me to make contacts with supply houses and obtain a line of credit. I had the usual struggle in building my business from 1890 to 1900 when, with Rufino's financial help, I purchased my first shop lot 100 feet square on the corner of Broadway and Scott where the Roskruge Hotel is now located.

On my return from California in 1888, and after my father's death on March 2 of 1889, some of my friends expressed a desire to form a group to meet in the evenings and take music lessons. We had Rufino Vélez, who was a lover of music and always ready for a good time. He knew not a note but he had, (like many Spaniards), a beautiful tenor voice of great power. Also in the group were Samaniego, Henry Levin, Villaescusa, my brother Dick, Tom Legarra, Lucas Estrella, and Santos Aros. I gave them all a few lessons in the rudiments of music. Dick was a good flutist, Henry could play a little on the violin, Santos Aros had played guitar by ear, and Samaniego had played flute in his young days. We organized as a music club and subscribed enough money to purchase a bass violin, a cello, and a viola. I purchased a clarinet, Rufino a trombone, Villaescusa a baritone, and Samaniego a flute. Dick got a cornet and we started teaching notes and the use of these instruments to the members. Samaniego dropped out and Dick took over the flute. Tom Legarra and Henry Levin had their own violins.

Any printed music of the very easy grades was too insipid and I got the idea of arranging some that could be played more effectively, giving the melodies and counterparts to Dick and Levin, Legarra and myself. In a few months we had a repertoire of danzas, mazurkas, polkas, songs and serenades that I had arranged, easy to play and pleasing melodies and simple harmonies to treat our friends.

Some of the Tucson music lovers suggested to us to get band instruments for a larger group and play weekly concerts at the Court plaza. A Mrs. Strauss (a good pianist) offered to raise the necessary funds to buy the larger instruments like tubas, drums, trombones, and altos. They brought us $300.00 and the rest of the money was used to build a band stand at the Court plaza. Some of the boys owned their own instruments and we all subscribed enough to buy a quartet of saxophones. We called the club, *Club Filarmónico Tucson- ense.*[13]

We played once a week at the plaza for nine years. Always had a good audience. In the summer we would play Wednes- day evenings, and Sunday afternoons in the winter months. Once every year we would play a concert at Reid's Opera House for the benefit of the St. Vincent de Paul Society. These concerts and promenade dances would net over a thousand dollars. We would play for church socials, National Holidays, Christmas, and New Year's festivities, dances for our friends, and serenades gratis.

We would exact pay from political meetings and parades and that would go into the band treasury. When we had accu- mulated several hundred dollars, we made a tour to Los Ange- les, Santa Barbara, Santa Monica, and Redondo (Calif.). The S.P.R.R. gave us reduced rates and all our band boys had a wonderful time at the expense of the band. By that time we had 30 members. Carlos Jácome, Alex Barreda, Filiberto Baffert, Genaro Manzo, Ed Rochester, Joaquín Legarra, Solly Drachman, Pete Grijalva, and others had joined. We had bought two sets of uniforms and we were really an important institution in Tucson.

One time we went to Nogales to celebrate a National holiday and remained there three days. We used to play for the dress parades of the Arizona National Guard and, before the Spanish-American War, our entire band joined the National Guard under Col. John Martin. At that time the officers were John Black, Emanuel Drachman, Frank Stevens, Willard Wright and others. I was appointed Band Leader with the rank of Sergeant Major. We used to have reviews and parades at the Military Plaza, about where the Santa Rita Hotel is now, and extending to the Carnegie Library and east to Fifth Avenue.

We were having a dress parade at the Military Plaza the Sunday when the news came that Admiral Dewey had destroyed the Spanish fleet and taken Manila. The war was practically ended and the Arizona National Guard was never called for active service. Some time after that, the pressure of my own business compelled me to resign. The band was kept together for a time but gradually disbanded. The Arizona State instruments and uniforms were turned over to Col. Martin and the instruments that belonged to the club were distributed to the old members. Also a lot of band and orchestra music [was divided among them], including all the books that I had written for the original orchestra. Manuel Montijo was known to have salvaged most of the music. His daughter Lolita (Mrs. Aros) told me that when her father had died after marrying the second time the widow, who knew nothing about music, had burned boxes of music left in the home and no doubt several hundred dollars worth of the Club Filarmónico's band music, including my own arrangements, went up in smoke.

During the life of the *Club Filarmónico* and before and after, I was identified with local musicians in home groups, church quartets, and others. I played many times with Mr. and Mrs. A. V. Grosetta, Mrs. Santiago Ainsa, Miss Marie Hittinger, later with Mrs. Sam Heineman, the Cathedral and All Saints Choirs. For the past ten years I have not even played at home. So my musical days are over. I still play little harmonies on the guitar for songs at home, but my love for good music is even greater now than ever.

One of the few old members of the *Club Filarmónico* gave Mr. Sewell two of my old books that he very kindly brought to me. So I have a good number of the melodies I wrote in my early twenties. We have a piano at home. I know the keyboard. I pick some of the old pieces that we had fifty years ago for my wife to hear them. In music paper and pencil that I keep on the piano I have jotted down strains and fragments to remind me of several of the old pieces that were never published and are now lost. I hope to have time some day to write many danzas, mazurkas, schottisches, polkas, waltzes and songs of the old days, many of them real good music.

[One] time a music teacher, Juan Balderas who played in our band, came in to show me a copy of piano music which one of his pupils had given to him. It looked yellowish and aged. The name on the cover was "*Sirvase Ud. Pasar*" [Please Come In] published by Wagner & Levin of Mexico City. The Music was a march written in 2-4 time, exactly the counterpart of *Washington Post March* written by John Philip Sousa, the well known band master of Washington. The *Washington Post March* had made a tremendous hit and Sousa was making a fortune out of it. Balderas thought that the same march, only in 2/4 in place of 6/8 time, had been published in Mexico years before under the name of *Sirvase Ud. Pasar* and the name of the composer had not been printed in the copy.

While we were looking over the sheet, a young reporter of the *Arizona Star* came by and stopped as he used to do many times when passing by the shop. He was a friend of mine and joined in the comments regarding the music. I could not believe that John Philip Sousa could have used some one else's music to publish it as his own, but the thing was puzzling. I suggested to Balderas to write to Wagner and Levin and forgot all about it.

A few days later I received a copy of the "*Musical Courier*" published in New York with a paragraph copied from a Tucson newspaper relating that I had seen this *Sirvase Ud. Pasar* music sheet the almost identical Sousa march. The *Star* reporter had written a short ten or fifteen line news item about it and the New York magazine had copied it. It caused a bombshell in musical circles until Wagner and Levin of Mexico City gave the lame explanation that they had used the popular march as a souvenir to their patrons on the opening of their new store building. They had published this march for piano and whoever wrote the manuscript for them had forgotten the name of the march as well as the name of the composer.

The next thing was a short stereotyped article relating the incident and ending by saying that all the excitement had occurred simply because Mein Herr Ronstadt, a country band leader in Arizona, could not read Spanish.

Epilogue

Bernard L. Fontana

The career of "this country band leader in Arizona" after the death of his father in 1889 has been briefly outlined by his son Edward in the introduction.

It would be impossible to overstate the impact of Fred Ronstadt and his siblings on the economic, social, and political life of southern Arizona. In addition to his accomplishments listed in the introduction, Fred was active as a Democrat in local politics and was once elected to serve a two-year term on the Pima County Board of Supervisors. He also supported for political office candidates who opposed gambling and allowing women in saloons and who favored higher licensing fees for saloon owners. "The political control in Tucson and Pima County in those days," he wrote, "was in the hands of saloon men and the gambling houses. While many of them men engaged in that line of business were good citizens, their following and the atmosphere surrounding them was bad."

More telling yet was his support of persons who campaigned against the American Protective Association (APA), an anti-

Catholic organization begun in 1887 with a Tucson chapter founded in 1894. The APA pandered to prejudice against certain classes of "foreigners," targeting especially Central and Eastern European immigrants who, it was pointed out, were largely Catholic. In the Southwest, Mexicans were the principal object of the APA's scorn.

Working within the Republican party, the APA's members were most successful between 1891 and 1896 in getting their candidates elected, especially during the depression of 1894.

The *Alianza Hispano-Americana* was formed in Tucson in 1894 by a group of Tucson's Mexican middle-class community to combat such views as those held by followers of the APA, and while Fred Ronstadt was not a founder, he joined the *aliancistas* in their efforts to counter negative stereotypes.[1]

Ronstadt was invited at various times to run for the territorial assembly, mayor's office, city council, and the state Senate—all of which he declined for business and personal reasons.

With his brother José María "Pepe" Ronstadt, it was another matter. Fred tells the story:

> The year that Woodrow Wilson was elected President (1913), Pepe had managed the Democratic campaign in Pima County very efficiently and later was appointed postmaster [of Tucson] by President Wilson and served with credit for eight years. He had also engaged in the cattle business and made a fine success in all his deals. He had stock in the Southern Arizona Bank and was a Director for several years until he died [of a heart

ailment in May 1933]. A few years before he died, he was elected Supervisor for Pima County. During his term as Chairman of the Board [1926–1928] he worked to build the [Pima County court house].

Pepe Ronstadt was also founder in 1903 of the Santa Margarita Cattle Company with its ranch headquarters just north of the Mexican border in the upper Altar Valley. This and other cattle holdings soon ranked him among the largest cattlemen in southern Arizona.

Pepe Ronstadt led the way for his older brother in marrying into the Zamorano-Wolfskill-Dalton extended family, whose roots lay in Mexican Southern California. Again, it is Fred who tells the story:

My mother and myself had been much concerned about Pepe's interest in a girl that we did not like for a relative-in-law. I could not help thinking that when Mr. Dalton's family would return to Tucson, Pepe would be attracted by one of the Dalton girls, all of whom we admired very much, and I personally know them not only to be beautiful and intelligent but of excellent breeding background.

The very day when Mr. Dalton's family came home from Los Angeles, Pepe brought Hortense [Dalton] and [her sister] Lupe to the [F. Ronstadt Company] office and the store to show them where and how we were working. I am sure that the contrast between the girl in whom he had been interested and the Daltons had impressed Pepe plenty. Before many days he and Hortense became more than friends and in less than a year they were married [1901].

Fred, who was then married to Sara Levin, had no way of knowing at the time that two years later he would become the husband of Lupe Dalton and that brothers would also become brothers-in-law.

Fred's brother Dick also went into the cattle business in southern Arizona as well as operating a store that sold hay, feed, wagons, and farm implements. He married Matilda Martin, daughter of Dr. George Martin, Sr., an Irish pharmacist who came to the United States in 1851, and of Delfina Redondo, daughter of José María Redondo of Sonora. Martin became one of the earliest druggists in Arizona, and his and Delfina Redondo's many descendants continue to exert a positive presence in the economic and social life of southern Arizona.[2]

Fred's sister Emilia married Jesús María Zepeda. Their daughter, Fresia, in turn married Robert Wood, Jr. For many years the Woods operated the old Zepeda family ranch in northern Sonora, the Garrapata, located a short distance south of the international boundary at Sasabe and not far from the Santa Margarita Ranch in the Arizona portion of the upper Altar Valley.

Pepe's and Hortense's son Carlos Edward was born in Tucson on August 25, 1903. Before he died in 1972, Carlos Ronstadt became one of southern Arizona's most prominent cattlemen and businessmen. Before Pepe died in 1933, he and Carlos organized the Baboquivari Cattle Company. After his father's death, Carlos and his mother Hortense took over operation of the Santa Margarita. He sold the north end of this "home" ranch and bought the Agua Linda Ranch south of Tucson in its place.

Carlos became a pioneer in the frozen food business in Arizona and formed Tucson Beef Feeders. He helped start the Erly-Fat Livestock Feed Company, served once as president of the Arizona Cattle Growers' Association, and was an executive committee member of the American National Cattlemen's Association. He was also a director of the Tucson Gas, Electric Light and Power Company, the Arizona Livestock Credit Production Association, and the Southern Arizona Bank.

Carlos's son, Karl Ronstadt, went into the construction business. Between 1972 and 1974 his construction company built the Tat Momolikat Dam on southern Arizona's Papago Indian Reservation—the sixth largest earthen dam in the world.

Of the one son and three daughters by Fred Ronstadt's marriage to Sara Levin, the best known was Luisa Espinel (see pp. xix–xx). Born in Tucson in 1892, she became a singer and dancer who earned international critical and popular acclaim.

Luisa grew up in a house full of music, her father the leader of the *Club Filarmónico,* one of Tucson's earliest and most famous orchestras. As a young woman, she often appeared for the

Saturday Morning Musical Club and even starred in a local production of the opera *Il Trovatore* directed by Professor José Servín in 1917. But her love of music, and her desire to make a profession of it, took her far from Tucson—first to San Francisco, and then to New York, Paris, and Madrid. Nevertheless, Luisa's Tucson childhood remained a personal touchstone throughout her career.[3]

In 1946, as a tribute to her father, Luisa published *Canciones de Mi Padre,* a collection of Mexican folk songs. Her niece, Linda Ronstadt, would perform and record a similar collection under the same title for her father in 1987.

Of Fred's four children with Lupe Dalton, all of them boys, Gilbert and Edward were the two who remained in southern Arizona throughout their lives and who managed the affairs of the F. Ronstadt Company until turning it over to two of their sons in 1983.

Gilbert married Ruth Mary Copeman, and one of their daughters, Linda, has become an internationally renowned singer. She began her recording career in 1967, has appeared in films, and has performed in *Pirates of Penzance* as well as in *La Bohéme.* She is a recipient of the American Music Award, Grammy awards, an Emmy award, and the Academy of Country Music Award.

One of Gilbert and Ruth Mary's sons, Peter Ronstadt, served as Tucson Chief of Police from 1981 until his retirement in 1992.

Edward Ronstadt married Mary Catherine Geis, and they have twelve children. In the continuing Ronstadt tradition of public service, one of their sons, James Frederick, has been director of the Tucson City Parks and Recreation Department since 1978.

Frederick Augustus Ronstadt of Hanover, Germany could not have dreamed that his sojourn to northern Mexico would eventually bear such fruit. His immediate offspring and their many descendants have become exemplars of what is good in the culture of the Borderlands—a region made special through its unique blending of peoples and traditions. Were Federico José María Ronstadt still alive, he would be terribly pleased.

Notes

Foreword

1. For details concerning the lives of these two men, see Rodolfo Acuña, *Sonoran Strongman: Ignacio Pesqueira and His Times* (Tucson: The University of Arizona Press, 1974), and Francisco R. Almada, *Diccionario de historia, geografía y biografía sonorenses* (N.p.: Chihuahua, 1952), 288–94 and 574–83.

2. Stuart F. Voss, *On the Periphery of Nineteenth-Century Mexico: Sonora and Sinaloa, 1810–1877* (Tucson: The University of Arizona Press, 1982), 284–87.

Introduction

1. Thomas Sheridan, "From Luisa Espinel to Lalo Guerrero: Tucson's Mexican Musicians Before World War II," *Journal of Arizona History* 25 (Autumn 1984), 287, 289.

2. Quoted in Sheridan, "From Luisa Espinel to Lalo Guerrero," 287. Sheridan also writes about Luisa Espinel in *Los Tucsonenses: The Mexican Community in Tucson, 1854–1941* (Tucson: The University of Arizona Press, 1986), 188–191.

3. Susanna B. Dakin, *A Scotch Paisano in Old Los Angeles: Hugo Reid's Life in California, 1832–1852, Derived from His Correspondence* (Berkeley: University of California Press, 1978), 119, 147, 300. For Agustín Zamorano, see James D. Hart, *A Companion to California,* rev. ed. (Berkeley: University of California Press, 1987), 576.

4. See Lloyd C. Engelbrecht, *Henry C. Trost: Architect of the Southwest* (El Paso, Texas: El Paso Public Library, 1981). The Ronstadt house is described on page 20.

5. A well-illustrated and detailed history of the F. Ronstadt Company and its wagon-making operations, one which includes extensive quotations from Fred Ronstadt's memoirs, is by James E. Sherman and Edward F. Ronstadt, "Wagon Making in Southern Arizona," *The Smoke Signal,* no. 31 (Spring 1975), 1–20.

Chapter 1

1. With the initial backing of Napoleon III, the Austrian archduke, Ferdinand Maximilian of Hapsburg, was emperor of Mexico from his arrival there in May 1864 until his execution by the Mexican forces of Benito Juárez in June 1867. See Michael C. Meyer and William L. Sherman, *The Course of Mexican History,* 3rd edition (New York: Oxford University Press, 1987), 391–401.

2. The story of Crabb's ill-fated effort to establish himself as a political power in Sonora is related in Robert H. Forbes, *Crabb's Filibustering Expedition into Sonora, 1857* (Tucson: Arizona Silhouettes, 1952).

3. I'll see you tonight,
Hidden from your uncle.
Let me know if you're awake
When I signal you 'psst.'

4. Colonel Altamirano, leading the state troops in support of Governor Ignacio Pesqueira, defeated the rebels led by Francisco Serna on August 23, 1875, at Altar. See Rodolfo F. Acuña, *Sonoran Strongman: Ignacio Pesqueira and His Times* (Tucson: The University of Arizona Press, 1974), 125). Also see pp. xi, 13–14 of this book.

5. See pp. xvii–xviii above.

Chapter 2

1. The United States–Mexico Boundary was surveyed and marked here in 1855. It was the construction of the New Mexico and Arizona Railroad through Calabasas in 1882 that led speculators to predict a boom for the site. The details are in David F. Myrick, *The Railroads of Arizona,* vol. 1, *The Southern Roads* (Berkeley: Howell-North, 1975), 279–81.

2. A colorful version of Pete Kitchen's Arizona career is in Gil Procter, *Tucson, Tubac, Tumacacori, Tohell: The Trails of Pete Kitchen* (Tucson: Dale S. King, 1964).

3. See Bernard L. Fontana, "Calabazas of the Río Rico," *The Smoke Signal,* no. 24 (Fall 1971), 85.

4. See William F. Hogan, "Adolph George Buttner: Tucson's First Chief of Police," *Arizoniana* 5, no. 2 (Summer 1964), 26–31.

5. The story of the original St. Augustine Cathedral is told in George W. Chambers and C. L. Sonnichsen, *San Agustín Church in Arizona* (Tucson: Arizona Historical Society, 1974). The "cut stone entrance" now adorns the entrance to the Arizona Historical Society headquarters in Tucson.

6. I give you praise and thanks, great Lord, and I praise your great power, for you have allowed me to awaken with my soul still in my body. I ask you, my Creator, in your charity and love, to allow me to reach the

evening in Your grace and service forevermore. Amen. Guardian angel, amiable companion, do not abandon me this night or during the day. I lay me down with God and I get up with God. God with me and I with Him; God before me and I behind Him.

7. See p. xviii.

8. A more up-to-date interpretation, and by far the best account of the Yaqui Easter ceremonies, is to be found in Muriel T. Painter, *With Good Heart: Yaqui Beliefs and Ceremonies in Pascua Village* (Tucson: The University of Arizona Press, 1986).

9. See Jack S. Williams, "San Augustin [*sic*] del Tucson: A Vanished Mission Community of the Pimeria [*sic*] Alta," *The Smoke Signal,* nos. 47–48 (Spring–Fall 1986), 113–128.

10. See Dakin, *A Scotch Paisano,* 119, 147, 300; Hart, *A Companion to California,* rev. ed., 576; and p. xx above.

11. Not actually a mission, this was the original Los Angeles parish church, Nuestra Señora de la Reina de Los Angeles de Porciúncula.

12. Luis María Wolfskill was the youngest son of William Wolfskill. He died in 1884 at the age of 36. He and Luisa had seven children: Alice, Frank, Herbert, Isabel, Julian, William, and one who died in infancy. See Iris H. Wilson, *William Wolfskill, 1798–1866* (Glendale, California: The Arthur H. Clark Co., 1965), 113.

13. This was one of Tucson's "earliest and most famous orchestras." See Sheridan, *Los Tucsonenses,* 190.

Epilogue

1. Thomas Sheridan, *Los Tucsonenses: The Mexican Community in Tucson, 1854–1941* (Tucson: The University of Arizona Press, 1986), 111, 117, 283 n. 40.

2. See Armand Martin Ronstadt, "Dr. George Martin, Sr., Pioneer Arizona and Tucson Druggist, Founder of the Martin Drug Company," *The Smoke Signal,* no. 56 (Fall 1991), 101–120.

3. Sheridan, *Los Tucsonenses,* 190.

Bibliography

Acuña, Rodolfo F. *Sonoran Strongman: Ignacio Pesqueira and His Times.* Tucson: The University of Arizona Press, 1974.

Almada, Francisco R. *Diccionario de historia, geografía y biografía sonorenses.* N.p.: Chihuahua, 1952.

Chambers, George W., and C. L. Sonnichsen. *San Agustín: First Cathedral Church in Arizona.* Tucson: Arizona Historical Society, 1974.

Dakin, Susanna B. *A Scotch Paisano in Old Los Angeles: Hugo Reid's Life in California, 1832–1852, Derived from His Correspondence.* Berkeley: University of California Press, 1978.

Engelbrecht, Lloyd C. *Henry C. Trost: Architect of the Southwest.* El Paso, Texas: El Paso Public Library, 1981.

Bernard L. Fontana. "Calabazas of the Rio Rico." *The Smoke Signal,* no. 24 (Fall 1971), 65–88.

Forbes, Robert H. *Crabb's Filibustering Expedition into Sonora, 1857.* Tucson: Arizona Silhouettes, 1952.

Hogan, William F. "Adolf George Buttner: Tucson's First Chief of Police." *Arizoniana* 5, no. 2 (Summer 1964), 26–31.

Hart, James D. *A Companion to California.* Rev. ed. Berkeley: University of California Press, 1987.

Meyer, Michael C., and William L. Sherman. *The Course of Mexican History.* 3rd edition. New York: Oxford University Press, 1987.

Myrick, David F. *The Railroads of Arizona.* Vol. 1. *The Southern Roads.* Berkeley: Howell-North, 1975.

Painter, Muriel Thayer. *With Good Heart: Yaqui Beliefs and Ceremonies in Pascua Village.* Tucson: The University of Arizona Press, 1986.

Procter, Gil. *Tucson, Tubac, Tumacacori, Tohell: The Trails of Pete Kitchen.* Tucson: Dale S. King, 1964.

Ronstadt, Armand Martin. "Dr. George Martin, Sr., Pioneer Arizona and Tucson Druggist, Founder of the Martin Drug Company." *The Smoke Signal,* no. 56 (Fall 1991), 101–120.

Sheridan, Thomas. "From Luisa Espinel to Lalo Guerrero: Tucson's Mexican Musicians Before World War II." *Journal of Arizona History* 25 (Autumn 1984) 285–300.

———. *Los Tucsonenses: The Mexican Community in Tucson, 1854–1941.* Tucson: The University of Arizona Press, 1986.

Sherman, James E., and Edward F. Ronstadt. "Wagon Making in Southern Arizona." *The Smoke Signal,* no. 31 (Spring 1975), 1–20.

Voss, Stuart F. *On the Periphery of Nineteenth-Century Mexico: Sonora and Sinaloa, 1810–1877.* Tucson: The University of Arizona Press, 1982.

Williams, Jack S. "San Augustin [*sic*] del Tucson: A Vanished Mission Community of the Pimeria [*sic*] Alta." *The Smoke Signal,* nos. 47–48 (Spring-Fall 1986), 113–128.

Wilson, Iris H. *William Wolfskill, 1798–1866.* Glendale, California: The Arthur H. Clark Co., 1965.

Acknowledgments

I would like to thank several people who helped the compiling and editing of my father's memoirs. Bernard L. Fontana, known as Bunny to his friends and associates, was an invaluable advisor and aide in the process of producing the manuscript for *Borderman*. A boon companion on numerous trips into Sonora, James M. Murphy was my and Bunny's guide to the site where my father was born. And finally, I want to thank Joe Wilder and his staff at the University of Arizona Southwest Center for their moral and monetary support for the publication of *Borderman*.

EDWARD F. RONSTADT
Tucson, Arizona

Index

149

Borderman
was designed by Emmy Ezzell
and composed on a 486 PC clone using Aldus PageMaker 4.0,
with Adobe Garamond fonts and Wood Type ornaments.
The jacket was designed by Harold Augustus on CorelDraw,
and printed by Thomson-Shore, Inc.
using film made by American Color Inc.
Don Bufkin drew the maps.
The book was printed and bound by Thomson-Shore, Inc.
on acid-free Glatfelter paper.